A GUIDE TO EARLY YEARS PRACTICE

Sandra Smidt

London and New York

First published 1998
by Routledge
11 New Fetter Lane, London EC4P 4EE

© 1998 Sandra Smidt

Typeset in Garamond by BC Typesetting, Bristol
Printed and bound in Great Britain by
Page Bros (Norwich) Ltd

British Library Cataloguing in Publication Data
A catalogue record for this book is available from the British Library

Library of Congress Cataloguing in Publication Data
Smidt, Sandra, 1943–
Guide to early ears practice/Sandra Smidt.
p.   cm.
Includes bibliographical references and index.
ISBN 0–415–16961–5 (pb : alk. paper)
1. Early childhood education–Great Britain.   2. Child
development–Great Britain.   I. Title.
LB1139.3.G7S65   1998
371.212'0941–dc21   97-43224
                                            CIP

ISBN 0–415–16961–5

For Hannah, Ben and the May baby

CONTENTS

1

UNDERSTANDING HOW YOUNG CHILDREN LEARN BEST

Michael Chung is four years old. He goes to playgroup four mornings a week. At home his family speak Cantonese and English and Michael is fluent in both languages. One morning Michael arrives at playgroup. He takes off his coat and hangs it on his peg. He greets all the adults and heads straight for the home corner. He selects a doll, carefully undresses the doll and then places the doll in a plastic bucket of water in order to bath her. He holds the doll in one arm whilst he pretends to squeeze shampoo from an empty bottle on the doll's head. He rubs the head gently, using one hand to shield the doll's eyes and all the time he talks to the doll in a crooning voice, saying things like 'Don't cry. It will be all right. It will be nice and clean'. When he is satisfied that the doll is clean he lifts her out of the water, wraps her in a towel and starts to dress her. First he puts on a disposable nappy, then a vest, then a 'babygro'. That done, he picks up an empty feeding bottle and begins to feed the baby, this time singing to her. Finally, he puts the doll on his shoulder, pats her back and puts her down in a box which serves as a cot. Then he leaves the home corner, and goes over to a table where writing materials have been set out. He selects a blank booklet and begins to make marks on the pages, working from the front of the booklet to the back. Finally he takes a pencil and carefully writes his name on the front of the booklet and places it in the pocket of his coat to take home.

An everyday event in any playgroup, nursery or group. Nothing that Michael did was remarkable or surprising and most people observing Michael would have said that he was playing in the way most young children play. But this little vignette tells us quite a lot about Michael and gives us an insight into what he already knows, what he can do, what he is interested in and how he chooses to spend his time. Information like this is essential to anyone working with young children.

In this opening chapter we will look at what is currently known about how young children learn – and, most crucially, we will examine theories about how young children learn best. We do know that young children can be taught to do many things in many different ways. Our concern is to examine the best ways to promote learning in young children.

WHAT WE MEAN BY LEARNING

'Learning' is a word we all use frequently and often without really considering what it means. It is a word we use to describe an enormous range of experiences and events. To illustrate this, consider these statements:

'I learned, early on, that I wanted to be famous'
'Children learn through play'
'When I first learned to read I couldn't get enough books'
'Jamie learned to talk at nine months'
'I learned to drive'
'At school I had to learn poetry off by heart'
'I never learned another language'
'I used to hate olives, but then I learned to love them'

If you analyse each of these you will find that we sometimes use the word learning to talk about how we acquire skills – learning to drive, to walk or to use a knife and fork, for example. We use the word to talk about how we acquire attitudes – learning to enjoy the books or appreciate the taste of olives. We use the word to describe how we appreciate how to relate to other people. In short, the word 'learning' is a broad term that defines what happens to us in a range of circumstances and over an indefinite period of time. You will know that children learn at home, in the playground, at school, in the streets. Learning happens all the time.

What is actually happening when we learn is that connections between cells in the brain are laid down and strengthened. So 'learning' also has a very precise meaning. At birth, the human infant has all the brain cells needed for human development. In order for the human being to function, however, connections or pathways need to be formed between these cells. You will have read that learning during the first five years of life is more rapid than at any other time. This is why the early years of life are so crucial in terms of learning. Research has shown that these neural pathways are formed most effectively through experience. Each time a child encounters something new and interesting the child explores the new object or situation and as he or she does, connections between brain cells are laid down. If you are particularly interested in this you might like to try reading *Fertile Minds* written by Madeline Nash.

Let us pause at this point and return to the case study of Michael which opened this chapter.

Write down all the things you have learned in the past four years. Now write down all the things that Michael has learned in the past four years.

Your list might have included things like:

- learned to make meringues
- learned to use an electric drill
- learned to tango

In the list of what Michael has learned you might have included things like:

- learned to sit
- learned to stand
- learned to walk
- learned to use both hands in conjunction
- learned to understand and speak two languages
- learned how to bath a baby
- learned how to use a pencil
- learned how to behave at playgroup

You will realise from this just how accelerated learning is in the first few years of life. As we get older we do continue learning, but the rate decreases dramatically.

So we have established that learning means something very precise in terms of what happens physiologically. Many researchers and theorists have studied the development of children and their work is useful to those of us working with young children as it gives us a framework in which to plan our work. It also helps us to justify what we do to parents and to other workers. We will start by looking at some of the things the most influential theorists have to say and later in this book we will refer to them to support what we are saying.

The work of Jean Piaget

We will start by looking at the work of Jean Piaget, a Swiss theorist who studied his own children and children in groups. His work is important for a number of reasons. In the first place, he was the first person to show that the human infant is not passive, but actively tries to get meaning from all the experiences he or she encounters. Prior to this, people had believed that the infant had to be 'fed' experiences, but Piaget showed that the human infant is an 'active learner'. Many people, when they first encounter this idea, think it refers to the fact that the infant is physically active and

3

learns through this. Piaget meant, however, that the human infant is mentally or cognitively active. In other words, the human infant is busy trying to understand the world and each experience results in changes in mental function.

To explain this Piaget used the terms 'accommodation' and 'assimilation'. Assimilation is seen as the process of taking in new information, of adding to the existing experiences and sometimes changing these. Remember that all of this happens in the brain. Accommodation is the next stage of learning and is when the child or infant uses information in the brain in order to adapt to the environment. You will realise from this that Piaget saw accommodation as the higher order cognitive process, the one that allows us to solve problems.

The second reason for looking at the work of Piaget is that his work has had a profound effect on the school system in England. In his work he speculated that all children passed through clearly defined stages of development. The first stage, which he called the Sensorimotor stage, lasted from birth to the age of two. The second stage – which he called the stage of Pre-operational Thought – lasted from two to about seven. The stage of Operational Thought followed and was thought to continue to the age of about eleven. The final stage, that of Formal Operations, continued into adulthood. You will realise that these stages correspond closely with the English schools system: Nursery/ Infant from three to seven; Junior from eight to eleven; Secondary from eleven to adulthood.

Now it is important to note that, although Piaget's work was very important and influential, much of it has been criticised and the largest body of criticism relates to this stage theory of development. At first glance you may think that what you have read so far makes sense. To anyone involved with children it is clear that children do develop and that the behaviour and learning of a 7 year old is very different from that of a 3 year old. Piaget, however, tended to focus on what children could not yet do rather than looking at what they could do.

Let us take an example and analyse it to see what it tells us about what the child can do and about what the child cannot do yet.

> Four-year-old Rehana paints a picture at the easel, takes a pencil and makes some marks in the top right hand corner of the page. The first mark is clearly an attempt at the 'R' with which her name begins.

If you were considering what she knows you might say that she knows that she ought to write her name on her painting and that she knows the first letter of her name. If you were considering what she doesn't yet know you might say that she doesn't yet know how to write her name properly. For those of us working with children it is much more important to know what children already know and can do. This allows us to plan what to offer the child next in order to help them take the next step in learning.

In devising the stages Piaget tended to focus on what children could not yet do. This is particularly true of children in the Pre-operational stage, which is the stage which most concerns us. According to Piaget children under the age of about seven are not able to think logically or to conserve ideas of number, length, capacity or volume. Piaget's theories about this stage came from a number of experiments he did with children where he gave them tasks to do. Many of these are well known, as, for example, giving children two identical lumps of plasticine and then dividing one lump into a number of smaller lumps. The child was then asked 'Are they the same?'. Younger children tended to answer that they were not the same, that the lump that had been divided up into several smaller lumps 'had more'. Some critics of Piaget point out that since the children had witnessed the adult dividing up one lump of plasticine, they must have assumed that this had to be a trick question. Other critics suggest that the children couldn't see the point of the activity or of the question and so tended to give the answer they thought the adult wanted to hear.

Piaget also said that young children in the Pre-operational stage are not able to take on the perspective of someone else. In other words, young children are what he called 'egocentric': they see themselves as being central to everything and cannot see the world from anyone else's point of view. He did not mean that young children are selfish, but that they cannot mentally put themselves into the position of someone else. To illustrate this he carried out an experiment involving three papier maché mountains. The young child was placed in front of these models and then a doll was put in a position offering a different view of the mountains. The children were asked to select the drawing which showed the view the doll could see. Very few of these young children were able to do this; they tended to select the picture showing the view they could see. For Piaget this was evidence enough.

How do you feel about this? Have you encountered young children who are able to demonstrate that they are able to appreciate what it feels like to be in someone else's shoes? How about the child who rushes over to comfort a friend who has fallen and grazed her knee?

Martin Hughes tried a different experiment to demonstrate that young children are able to take on the view of someone else. Children were told that a teddy had been naughty and were then asked to hide the teddy from a policeman doll. Many of the young children were able to do this. The reasons for this are both interesting and directly relevant to our work with young children. Hughes believed that these young children were able to 'decentre' (that is, to take on the views of another) when what they were asked to do made sense to them. He also believed that young children demonstrate what they know best when they are able to draw on their previous experience. In his 'Naughty Teddy' experiment he felt that many of the young children had had experience of hiding things or of hiding themselves. They also might have had experience of being 'naughty' and could see why the teddy might need to be hidden from the policeman.

A pause now, to draw breath and to pull out the two main themes of this section:

- From birth, human infants actively seek to understand their world.
- Young children learn best when they can see the purpose of what they are doing and when they are able to draw on their previous experience.

The work of Margaret Donaldson

Let us now turn to the work of a more recent theorist, Margaret Donaldson. She was one of Piaget's fiercest critics and the person who motivated Hughes in much of his research. In her book *Children's Minds*, published in 1978, she looked at how children are taught when they first start school and related it to what was known about how young children learn. The learning children are required to do when they start formal schooling is what Donaldson called 'decontextualised', which means that it is not rooted in a context. Take, for example, children being asked to colour in a set of balloons on a worksheet. This is not something that is set in a context that makes sense to young children. Why are they being asked to do this? What purpose does it serve? Will it matter if the big balloon is red rather than blue? As a contrast you might like to consider the young child painting spontaneously at an easel and selecting which colours to use.

Abstract learning – which describes much of the learning children do at school – is very difficult for young learners. They need to be able to draw on their previous experience and to use practical tools and activities to help them make sense of what they are doing. Of course, all children do need to be able to cope with abstract learning. We would not expect children to go through life always needing physical props and lifelike activities in order to learn. The crucial point Donaldson makes is that children need to be led gradually and gently into abstract learning and that this will happen best if children are allowed a range of experiences in settings which are familiar and which make 'human sense' to them. Donaldson calls settings like these 'meaningful contexts'.

To illustrate this more clearly let us examine some familiar activities which can be described as meaningful contexts:

> The children in the playgroup are baking cookies with an adult. They have been to the shops in order to buy the ingredients and one child handed over the money to the shopkeeper and got the change. The adult had a shopping list and had told the children what ingredients they would need. Back in the playgroup each child has a mixing bowl

and each is involved in beating together the ingredients, sifting the flour and spooning the mixture into cookie tins.

Can you see how this might be described as a 'meaningful context'?

All children will have had experience of going to the shops. They know that you need to buy things and that that involves some exchange of money. They have probably been to the shops with someone carrying a shopping list. Moreover, all children are familiar with food, with cooking and with eating. So it is an activity whose purpose is clear (delicious cookies to eat!) and one which is familiar.

> The staff in the nursery have set up a baby clinic in a corner of the room. Two children have recently had baby sisters. The clinic is equipped with some posters and leaflets obtained from the local baby clinic up the road, weighing scales, a baby bath, some dolls, some clipboards, a stethoscope donated by a parent and a doll's cot.

Can you see how this might be described as a 'meaningful context'?

Here again, many children will have had some experience of going to a clinic and those with younger siblings may have accompanied parents to the baby clinic.

It is easy to see how activities like this are both familiar and meaningful to children. What many people find difficult to understand (and sometimes to explain to parents) is what children are actually learning as they play in settings like these. In order to answer this question we need to look more closely at what we man by 'play'. Everyone working with young children knows that play is important. We often say things like 'Children learn through play' or 'Play is children's work'. But what do we mean by play and how can we be sure that play is so important in the early years?

THE IMPORTANCE OF PLAY

Many researchers and theorists have written about play. You may be familiar with the books by **Tina Bruce** or **Janet Moyles**. What is special about play is that it is something the child has chosen to do. So if you tell a child to go and play with the Lego, for example, the child has not chosen to do this and what the child does cannot properly be described as play. When a child has chosen to do something this indicates that the child is following some interest of his or her own. The child is then free to follow this interest and pursue it, often over a long period of time. Here is an example:

Hannah is 13 months old. She is playing outdoors with a plastic bowl of water, a paintbrush, a scrubbing brush, a sieve and a small container. The adults with her have shown her how to paint with water on the yard floor. Because, like most children, she is obliging she copies what the adults do for a few seconds. But her real interest lies elsewhere. She scuttles backwards and forwards between her mother and the plastic bowl, carrying both brushes in one hand. She hands the brushes to her mother, takes them back, returns to the bowl, places them in the water, takes them out, returns to her mother and so on. The activity lasts for more than 40 minutes.

It is difficult to know what Hannah is pursuing as she plays. Perhaps she is exploring the distance between the bowl and her mother. Perhaps it is perfecting the newly developed skill of holding two objects in one hand. But what is clear is that this is something in which she is deeply engrossed and that she pursues for a long period of time. We often hear people say that young children have a 'limited concentration span'. This is only true when children are doing things they have been told to do rather than things they have chosen to do.

Because children have chosen what they do when they play, they set their own goals. The second important feature of play is that it carries no risk of failure. The child has decided what to do and therefore cannot fail. No one has set the child goals that are too difficult or even too easy. The purpose of the play is in the child's hands.

A theorist who wrote a great deal about play was the Russian psychologist **Vygotsky**. He was particularly interested in two aspects of play. Firstly he believed that in play, particularly in imaginative play, children operate at their highest level of intellectual functioning, way beyond their everyday competence. He believed that, in play, a child stands 'a head taller' than him- or herself. What he meant by this was that when you observe a child engaged in imaginative play and pay close attention to what they are doing, they demonstrate knowledge and abilities that you would not see when the child is in a different situation. Here is an example to illustrate this:

Johan is in the reception class. He finds it difficult to do the tasks expected of him – writing, doing number work, colouring in and so on. But his teacher was surprised to notice that when he was out in the playground playing 'pirates' on the climbing frame he was able to express ideas, solve problems, communicate his thoughts and ideas and negotiate with the other children. In his imaginative play he stood a 'head taller' than he appeared in the classroom.

The second aspect of play that interested Vygotsky was how, through play, children begin to understand what is called 'the symbolic function'. A symbol is something that stands for or represents something else. Our spoken language is symbolic. The word 'dog' stands for or represents the living creature. Our written language is symbolic. The letters 'd-o-g' stand for that same living creature. Our number system is symbolic. The symbol '2' means more than one and less than three. In order to live in the real world all children need to come to understand how one thing can stand for another.

In imaginative play children, from very early on, begin to use one thing to represent another. The young child who places a block to her ear and pretends it is a telephone is doing just this. This experience of making one thing stand for another is a vital part of learning since many of the ways in which we describe and represent the world are symbolic. You have only to look around you and observe the written words, hear the sounds, notice the logos and pictures and numerals to realise how important this is. In order to learn to read and write, to talk, to build and draw, to count and measure and to communicate your thoughts and ideas, this knowledge is vital.

Another pause and time to draw out the main themes from these two sections:

- Abstract learning is difficult for young children who need a lot of experience of doing things, handling objects, and exploring the physical and social world.
- Children learn best in situations which make 'human sense' to them.
- Children learn best when they have chosen what to do – i.e. when they play.
- Through play children demonstrate all that they know. Observing children at play and paying close attention to what they are actually doing is our best way of understanding what they already know and are interested in.
- Through imaginative play children begin to understand how to use one thing to represent another – an essential skill in learning how to describe and communicate thoughts and ideas.

THE ROLE OF ADULTS

So far we have looked at what the children are doing and not made much mention of what the adults involved with young children do to support and extend their learning. Piaget believed that all that the adults working with young children needed to do was to provide them with an interesting and stimulating environment. This is important, of course. Children do need to encounter new and exciting activities and objects to explore. But some theorists have paid more attention to the role of adults and it is to their work we turn now.

Vygotsky was not only interested in play. Like Piaget, he saw the child as an active learner, but for him the context in which learning took place was vital. He was interested in how knowledge is passed on from one generation to another and, by definition, this implies that people around the child have an important role to play. Vygotsky viewed learning as an essentially social activity. Piaget was more interested in how children acquire knowledge and his view is thus more focused on the individual child than on the child in society.

Vygotsky believed that children are able to perform at a higher level when they are offered help than if left to struggle on their own. He called the gap between what a child could do unaided and what the child could do with help the 'Zone of Proximal Development'. It is important to understand that this is not something visible to the naked eye. It represents the child's potential. Perhaps an example will make this clear:

> Dana is pretending to write in the writing area of her nursery (Figure 1.1). The nursery nurse watching her notices that in her pretend writing are some letter shapes, including the D and the A from her name. The adult comments on the fact that Dana already knows how to write some of the letters in her name.

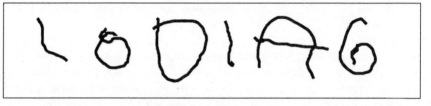

Figure 1.1 Dana's first attempt at writing her name. You can see that the 'D' and 'A' are included in her string of letter-like shapes.

> The next time Dana pretends to write (Figure 1.2) she again makes lots of marks and some letter-like shapes, but this time she says she is writing her name as she writes the D, the A and the N of her name.

Figure 1.2 Dana's second attempt at writing her name. This time you can see that, whilst she still includes a string of letter-like shapes, she has managed to write her name separately.

The adult, by paying careful attention to what Dana was doing, has helped Dana to develop from including some of the letters she knows from her name to writing her name recognisably. The adult has helped the child perform at a higher level, thus bridging the Zone of Proximal Development.

Jerome Bruner, another theorist who has studied the development of young children, describes what the adult has done in the above example as 'scaffolding' the child's learning. A scaffold is something that is erected to help builders gradually construct a building. Once the building is in place the scaffold is removed. Bruner believed that adults can allow children to take small, supported steps in their learning. When the learning is complete, the support of the adult is no longer needed.

In order to successfully scaffold learning the adult has to understand both what the child already knows and what the child is paying attention to. The worker in the above example guessed that Dana was interested in writing the letters of her own name. In this case she was right, but there is no guarantee. One way in which you know that you have been correct in your guess is by the child's response. Children quickly let you know when you are way off-beam!

Here is an example to show what happens when the adult follows his or her own agenda rather than successfully tuning in to what the child is paying attention to:

> Harinder, playing in the home corner, brings the playgroup worker a plastic plate on which she has placed some wooden blocks, some bits of plasticine and some beads. 'It's dinner' she announces 'sausages and beans and chips'.
>
> 'Oh, thank you!' replies the worker. 'How many sausages have you got? Can you count them?'
>
> Harinder picks up the plate and moves away.

The worker saw the opportunity to assess the child's knowledge of counting. But counting the sausages was not what Harinder was interested in. Her response was to walk away from the adult. Instead of her learning having been taken forward it was effectively stopped.

So it is important to try and understand the child's purposes. It is also important to start with what the child already knows. Scaffolding sometimes involves breaking down the task into smaller tasks; sometimes helping the child to become aware of what he or she has achieved; sometimes helping the child sequence what they are doing and sometimes helping the child focus on an aspect of the task which is relevant. These are things that many parents and workers do almost instinctively.

Scaffolding learning is a skill well worth developing. Here are some examples of adults scaffolding learning:

Joshua (aged 11 months) puts his empty bottle against the doll's face. His mother says 'Oh Josh! You are feeding the doll.'

Malindi (aged four years two months) is re-telling the story of 'We're going on a Bear Hunt' from the book and, by mistake, turns over two pages. The nursery worker comments on this and helps her find the right page, so that her re-telling of the story continues in the correct order.

Manna (aged four years, seven months) is working with junk materials and announces that she is making a microwave for her mother. She has gathered together a large number of boxes and containers and seems to have lost her way. The teacher suggests she starts off by selecting one box for the microwave. Once that is done she guides Manna in selecting the other materials she will need to complete her chosen task.

It should be clear from this that both Bruner and Vygotsky saw the role of adults as crucial. They saw the interaction between the child and adult as one of the most important features of any learning that takes place. When the adult intervenes in the learning situation, the interaction must be sensitive and the adult should not attempt to test the child or to stretch the child too far. To illustrate this, here are some examples. You might like to assess them to see if you feel that the adult's intervention fulfils the criteria laid out above:

'Louisa is nearly six. She has been working on making a boat out of junk materials. She has been experiencing difficulty in getting the materials to stick together.

"Oh I need some more glue" she said and put more glue on and held it tight. "If it doesn't work this time I'm not going to use it." As she let go of it, it fell off. She took it and threw it across the table in anger.

"What about using an elastic band?" I suggested. Louisa agreed and held the form in place while I put an elastic band over it.

"Good, it worked!" she said, looking at the other children. "That's good, isn't it, using an elastic band?".'

Susan Bragg (in Smidt (ed.) 1995)

'Two four year olds, Damian and Willy, are playing with magnets. Damian puts the magnets on the table. They attract. He then picks up one of the magnets and a wooden brick. Nothing happens. He tries with the glue pot. Again, nothing happens.

"It won't stick to the brick or the glass, but it sticks to the paper clip" I said and then added "I wonder why?"

Damian tries the sponge and then the metal sharpener. As the sharpener moves across the table towards the magnet Damian begins to laugh.

"That shoots down, look!"

He picks up the spoon.

"Yeah, a spoon'll stick and a knife. Both do stick to the magnet. It's a bit of a funny trick."

I then said "Some things did stick, but some didn't."

Later the boys are joined by three-year-old Ollie who asks "Do hands stick?"

He picks up one of the magnets and holds it against the palm of his hand.

Damian responds "No."

"Why?" asks Ollie.

"Because it hasn't got the thing – the magnet thing."

I repeat his response "The magnet thing?"

Damian goes on "The bit that sticks."'

Gerardine Lanigan (in Smidt (ed.) 1994)

You will have realised that in each example 'I' referred to the adult. You will also notice, in the second example, how the children were learning from one another. Vygotsky emphasised that children learn from one another and that more advanced children often provide models for younger children.

Let us now summarise the key points from this section:

- Adults have a key role to play in providing an environment which is stimulating and challenging.
- Adults need to understand what children already know and can do in order to help children develop and learn.
- Adults need to pay careful attention to what children are interested in or are paying attention to.
- Adults need to ensure that their intervention is sensitive and focused on the child's interests and not on their own agenda.
- Scaffolding children's learning helps children bridge the gap between what they can do alone and what they can do with help.

THE IMPORTANCE OF LANGUAGE IN LEARNING

You will remember that Piaget believed that the role of the adult was primarily to provide a stimulating and challenging environment in which children could learn. He saw language as a system of symbols for representing the world and as something quite separate from the actions which led to reasoning and the development of logical thinking. He believed that explaining things to small children, before they were 'ready' was a waste of time. Using words to help children make sense of situations led to children learning what have been called 'empty procedures'. This view of the adult use of language is held by certain practitioners today who believe in what is called 'heuristic play'. Young children are invited to explore new and interesting objects physically without the verbal intervention of adults. Supporters of this approach believe that this allows children to become deeply immersed in what they are doing and prevents them from being distracted by the adult intervention.

Vygotsky and Bruner, by contrast, both regard language as essential to learning. Much of Bruner's early research related to how adults help children acquire language. For him language involves much more than just talk. It includes gesture, inflection, intonation, body language and signs. Through the early turn-taking games that most primary care-givers play with their infants (things like 'Peekaboo') young children begin to use language both to communicate and to understand how language itself works. Young children begin to play with language just as they play with objects in the physical world. This verbal play, according to Bruner, is an essential component of development. You will have gathered already that Bruner also believed that adults, when scaffolding learning, use language to help the child make sense of the situation, to reflect on what they already know and can do and to take the next cognitive step.

Vygotsky paid particular attention to the development of speech and thought. He believed that these had different roots but later come together so that it is almost impossible to separate them out. Can you think without language? Can you talk without thinking? For young children speech is used at first to communicate, to make and share meanings. Later it becomes a tool of thought. By this he meant that language itself can change the way in which children think and learn.

In the earliest stages of speech Vygotsky believed that children go through a phase of talking aloud to themselves, explaining and describing what they are doing. This 'inner speech' serves to help children plan, control, recall and predict. You may have encountered young children's monologues and wondered what they were doing and why. As children get older this 'inner speech' becomes more abbreviated. Children no longer have to describe to themselves every step of what they are doing. The 'inner speech' becomes internalised as children become aware of what they are thinking. Children need to be aware of what they are thinking in order to learn.

This self-awareness comes partly through the internalisation of inner speech, but also through interactions with others. Adults often reflect back to children what they have said or done and in doing this they help children become aware of their own achievements. You can find evidence of this in the magnets example in the previous section. Where the adult draws the child's attention to something the child has done, the adult helps fill the gap between what the child can do alone and what the child can do with help – the Zone of Proximal Development. In other words, the adult allows the child to make conscious what he or she already knows and can do.

So children need both 'inner speech' and social speech (talking to and with others). Vygotsky believed that children learn first by trying to discover what something is or what it does through observing an experienced learner and learning from that. Then the child tries unaided, using 'inner speech' to explain the process. Learning is consolidated when the child internalises the concept.

Children encounter spoken language in all the activities they engage in at home. This applies to all children, whatever their backgrounds, cultures or languages. Parents, other family members, friends and carers use language as a normal part of everyday life. Every situation you can think of is bathed in language – cooking the supper, going to the bus, walking to the shops, digging in the garden and so on. Parents know what their children are interested in and they know what their children already know and what they can do and so they are tuned into their children's needs, interests and desires. The language within the home becomes a genuine dialogue with the parent sometimes listening to the child and the child sometimes listening to the parent.

In 1984 **Tizard and Hughes** studied the language used by the parents of young children and contrasted it with the language used by teachers once children started at school or nursery. There had previously been the notion that working-class parents tended to use an inferior form of language at home with their children, a form of language that did not allow the children to predict, to solve problems and to move away from the here and now in their thinking. The work of Tizard and Hughes (and a subsequent study by **Gordon Wells** (1987)) disproved this and showed that all parents, whatever their socioeconomic level, use language in order to make and share meaning and they thus enable their children to acquire language which allows them to think, to learn, to talk and to solve problems.

The failure of many poorer children in the school system cannot then be blamed on the language used within the home. What Tizard and Hughes found was that once children started school or nursery the language used by the adults was very different. Instead of engaging in genuine dialogue around life-like problems and situations, adults in schools tended to subtly test children, often trying to get the child to give the correct answer to questions.

Let us look at two examples, one set in a home and the other in a nursery class. As you read through them try and see how the language used by the adult either helps the child by scaffolding learning or inhibits learning by refusing to pay proper attention to the child's interests.

At home three-year-old Mpo is waiting for her tea with her sister Zinzi. Their mother slices and butters bread and spreads Marmite on it.

'Here, girls' she says as she brings the sandwiches to the table. 'I've cut each slice in half so you can have two each.'

'Two for me and two for you' says Mpo.

'That's four' says five-year-old Zinzi.

At nursery Mpo takes a piece of cardboard over to the teacher.

'Can you cut it in half for me?' she asks. 'The scissors are too hard for me.'

The teacher obliges and handing the two pieces of card back to the child asks 'And what have you got?'

Mpo looks baffled. The teacher repeats the question.

'Two?' suggests Mpo hopefully.

'Two what?' persists the teacher, determined that the child use the word 'half' in her response.

'Two . . . cards.'

You will notice that in the second example the child actually requests that the adult cut the card in half. Had the adult been paying proper attention to the child she would not have had to test the child as she did.

In this section, the key points are as follows:

- Language is vital for learning, although there may well be times when children are so deeply involved in what they are doing that the adult does not need to intervene verbally.
- Children learn from watching experienced learners, by using 'inner speech' and by internalising the concept.
- Children need both 'inner speech' and social speech.
- Language which involves a genuine dialogue and allows the child to be an equal participant is more likely to take learning forward than instructing, questioning and testing.

SO WHAT SHOULD YOUNG CHILDREN BE DOING?

We will now turn to the work of someone writing today. **Lillian Katz** has spent many years considering how young children learn best. She believes that we already know a great deal about how children learn and develop and that this knowledge should inform the curriculum we offer to young children. In her paper, called 'What should young children be learning'

(1988) she draws a distinction between what children can do and what children should do. She says:

> 'Just because children can do something when they are young does not mean that they should do it. . . . You can make children work for gold stars and tokens and all sorts of rewards, but that doesn't mean you should. What's interesting is that almost anything you get young children to do they appear to be willing to do. They don't appear to be suffering and some of then even look as though they love it.'

For Katz, the developmental question is not just *how* do children learn – because children always learn. Some children learn to lie, some to cheat, some to steal, some to read. The essential question is what is it that young children should be doing that will *best* serve their development in the long run?

Katz is not alone in believing that this is a crucial question facing educators and carers alike. Learning is about more than acquiring skills and knowledge: it involves both feelings and attitudes or what Katz calls 'dispositions'. A disposition can be defined as a habit of mind. You may have the disposition to be friendly or the disposition to be unfriendly. Almost all young children have the disposition to be curious. We have seen how children actively seek to make sense of the world and eagerly explore all new opportunities and experiences. Where children encounter inappropriate learning experiences there is a very real danger that this disposition – to be a learner – will be damaged.

At this point you might like to pause and consider what you think might be inappropriate learning experiences for young children.

What did you come up with? Theorists like Katz and **David Elkind** believe that where children encounter formal learning at too young an age they may learn the skills and knowledge required at that point, but their dispositions to be learners may be damaged. Elkind believes that children forced into formal learning too soon become less independent thinkers and tend to become very reliant on adults. They don't develop their abilities to be reflective learners or to be aware of what they can do and what they know. They are dependent on the adults around them to reward their efforts with praise, or gold stars or whatever system of approval operates in their playgroup or nursery. Such children may lose interest in what it is they are doing (the process) because all the approval they get relates to the end-product. They become like little workers on an assembly line, getting through their 'work' as quickly as possible so that they can then go on and do what really matters to them – that is, play. Children in such formal and inappropriate learning situations will not get deeply involved in what they are doing.

17

To summarise this section:

- Learning involves more than acquiring skills and knowledge: it also involves feelings and dispositions.
- What children do affects how they feel about themselves as learners.
- A too formal curriculum introduced at too early an age may result in children showing short-term gains in skills and knowledge, but long-term damage to their dispositions to be learners.
- Those working with young children should enable children to get deeply involved in what they are doing and, in interacting with children, should try to concentrate on what the children are doing rather than on any end-product.

A LAST WORD

In this introductory chapter we have looked briefly at what some of the theorists and researchers have said about how young children learn best. We have established that learning has a precise meaning – the establishment of connections between brain cells – and that this happens most efficiently where children are able to explore their world in as many ways as possible. Children are naturally curious and when they are encouraged to follow their own interests – that is, to play – they will become deeply involved and may spend a long time exploring something. This in-depth play is what educators are seeking to encourage in the early years.

We have explored the role of adults and seen that it involves not only providing a stimulating and challenging environment, but also interacting sensitively and in a way which is likely to help the child take the next step in learning and development. Interaction will be most supportive where the adult is able to tune in to what it is the child is interested in and in what the child is exploring. We have seen how important the role of language is in learning and how adults can use language to extend learning where they engage in genuine dialogue with children.

We have recognised that young children are very busy trying to make sense of their world. They learn by drawing on what they already know and have experienced, and need many experiences set in familiar and meaningful contexts to help them. In this way they are able to move towards being able to hold images and ideas in their heads and then to cope with the abstract learning that is required of them at school.

Many people believe that the younger you start teaching a child, the better the results will be. You will have encountered parents who eagerly teach their very young children to read and write. As Lillian Katz reminds us, young children are very obliging and will learn anything we teach them. But the consequences of such early formal learning may be negative in the long term. It is important to keep reminding ourselves that children in Britain start formal schooling at an earlier age than in any other developed country. Increasingly children are starting in the reception class at the age of only four. If these children are going to go on to be successful learners for life it is important that those working with them bear in mind the important and undisputed findings cited in this chapter.

REFERENCES

Bragg, S., 'Talk and Technology' in Smidt, S. (ed.) *'I Seed it and I Feeled it': Young Children Learning*, UNL Press, 1995.

Bruce, T., *Early Childhood Education*, Hodder and Stoughton, 1987.

Donaldson, M., *Children's Minds*, Fontana, 1978.

Elkind, D., 'Formal Education and Early Childhood Education: An Essential Difference', in *Phi Delta Kappa*, May 1986.

Katz, L., 'What Should Young Children Be Learning?' in *American Educator*, Summer 1988.

Lanigan, G., 'Children Playing with Magnets' in Smidt, S. (ed.) *'I Seed it and I Feeled it': Young Children Learning*, UNL Press, 1995.

Moyles, J., 'To Play or Not to Play? That is the Question' in Smidt, S. (ed.) *'I Seed it and I Feeled it': Young Children Learning*, UNL Press, 1995.

Moyles, J., *'Just Playing'*, OUP, 1989.

Nash, M., *Fertile Minds*, PCP, 1997.

Smidt, S. (ed.) *'I Seed it and I Feeled it': Young Children Learning*, UNL Press, 1995.

Sutherland, P., *Cognitive Development Today: Piaget and his Critics*, PCP, 1992.

Tizard, B. and Hughes, M., *Young Children Learning: Talking and Thinking at Home and at School*, Fontana, 1984.

Wells, G., *The Meaning Makers: Children Learning Language and Using Language to Learn*, Hodder and Stoughton, 1987.

2

HOW TO SUPPORT AND EXTEND
THE LEARNING OF YOUNG
CHILDREN

In the first chapter we examined some of the theories and research concerning how young children learn best. We touched on the role of the adult and, in this chapter, we will go into this in more detail. For those of us working with young children a sound understanding of how children learn is only of use to us if we are able to act on it in the settings we offer to children and their parents. We need to understand what we can do to ensure that children are learning and developing in these settings.

This chapter will be interactive in the sense that you will be given some case studies to read followed by some questions to answer. In this way you are invited to interact with what you read. Do attempt to have a go at answering the questions. In many cases you will find there is no right or wrong answer. A lot of what we do in our work is informed guesswork. This applies particularly where we are trying to focus on what the child is doing or what interest the child is following. The only person who knows the answer to this for sure is the child, and we have no way of getting inside the child's head. So we have to pay close attention, use what we know about how children learn and then make an educated guess.

Here is an example:

> Maria (who is four years old) is working in the technology area of her nursery. It is well equipped with both tools and materials. She spends a long time choosing the materials to use. She selects six corks, six milk bottle tops, and an egg carton. She sticks a cork in each space of the egg carton and then sticks a bottle top on top of each cork. She takes it over to the nursery nurse and proudly announces that she has made a typewriter.

What do you think Maria is particularly interested in? Have a guess.

There are a number of things you might have said. You might have said that Maria was particularly interested in the number 6, or that she was exploring the concept of one-to-one correspondence by putting one thing on top of another. Or you might even have said that she was interested in putting one thing inside of or on top of another, so perhaps she was exploring position.

We have no way of knowing for sure and the only way in which we can test out our guesses is to make some comment to the child and then assess her reaction. In the real situation from which the example was drawn, the nursery nurse said to Maria 'I see that you got six corks and six bottle tops and you stuck a cork in each of the six spaces of the egg carton'. Maria beamed at her and immediately decided to make another 'typewriter'. You might like to hazard a guess as to what the child's reaction might have been if the adult, instead of commenting on what she had achieved, had asked her to count the corks or bottle tops.

SETTING UP THE ENVIRONMENT

Piaget, you will remember, believed that the essential role of the adult was to provide a stimulating environment in which the child could learn and develop. This is certainly the starting point for good early years provision and one to which you have probably already paid a lot of attention. In this section we will explore what you might provide and how you can ensure that what you provide meets the learning needs of the children.

Not all children are in the fortunate position of Maria in the example above. Many children do not attend well-equipped nurseries, but find themselves in church halls, village halls, draughty rooms, upstairs in someone's front room in a block of flats or in the annex to the local community centre. Not all providers have limitless resources, so what you provide and how you provide it become even more important than they do in the well-funded centre.

There are certain fundamental things all providers should strive to offer. Not all are expensive and many can be found in the homes of parents or be gathered together from jumble sales or car boot sales. If you have parents who are handy and willing to offer their services they can help by making clothes or home corner furniture or a host of other things. Essentials include books, writing and drawing and painting materials, things to build with, sand and water, and things to encourage domestic and imaginative play.

Ideally your setting should strive to organise the materials, toys and equipment in such a way that children can make their own choices and be independent in their play. Not only does this fit well with what we have learned about how young children learn but it also releases you for more vital things than finding the scissors or getting the puzzle out of a cupboard. Try and find low storage units and organise your equipment into these. There are many produced by educational suppliers, but these are often expensive. Cheaper ways are just as good: things like baskets or plastic storage tubs. It is also a good idea both organisationally and educationally to make sure that each basket or tub is labelled with both word and picture. Doing this helps children know where to find and put things and introduces children to the written word in a meaningful context.

Here is how one playgroup organised its resources:

> We went out and bought a set of plastic containers and then invited the children to help us sort the toys out. They put Lego in one, the train set in another, the farm animals in a third and so on. I then sat with the children and wrote labels. The children were really interested in what I was doing and I noticed that they wrote their own labels for the next few days. Then I asked them to help me cut out pictures of the objects and stick these next to the name. Some children wanted to draw pictures of the toys and so some labels have got a word, a photograph and a child's drawing. We thought it was going to be absolute chaos the first time we set the containers out on the floor in the morning before the children arrived – and it was. But that only lasted for one or two mornings. After that the children settled down – I guess they realised that this was how things were going to be every day so they didn't have to rush from one container to another. Now they are much more able to choose what to do and often a child will come in, go straight to one container and spend the whole morning playing with great concentration. The other really good thing that has happened is that the children get much more involved in tidying up now. It is like a game for them and they are getting better and better at sorting things out.

Having organised your resources it is time to think about how to offer children learning activities in familiar and meaningful contexts. You will remember how important it is for young children to be able to build on their previous experience and to see the point of what they are doing. Situations, drawn from children's lives, can easily be set up in your group and will offer children important learning activities as they play. The most obvious of these is some sort of area where domestic play can take place – in other words, a home corner. Do remember that the homes children come from will vary and you will want to include in your home corner some artefacts and objects which will be familiar to the children in your group.

Here is one example:

> Our old home corner was very small and we found that the children were not really playing very well in it. We sat down after nursery one day and had a real go at working out what was going wrong. We decided that the children were bored with the things in there and we noticed that the boys hardly went in there at all and our Turkish

children would go in, play for a few seconds and then leave. So we decided to ask the parents to help out. The Turkish mothers brought in a Turkish coffee pot and some dressing up clothes. One mother brought in a Turkish newspaper. Then one of the black mothers commented that all our dolls were white, so we went out and bought a black doll. One of the staff thought about bringing in an old tool box and some 'Do It Yourself' magazines. We got the children to help us rearrange things to make the area bigger. Since then – and that is at least six months ago – the children have been playing in there with much greater concentration and we notice many more children doing things like pretending to read the newspapers or to write messages and playing many more roles while acting out complex sequences.

It seems obvious that where children encounter a range of materials to play with their play will become increasingly complex and engrossing. If you have things like knives and forks in your home corner do try and have complete sets of these – say four knives and four forks. This will help the children in their understanding of numbers and allow them to imitate some of the roles they see their families play at home. Do remember to reflect not only the range of cultures in your group but also to respect them. Not all families use knives and forks, for example. In some cultures food is eaten using the hands, in others people use tools like chopsticks.

In many settings workers try and extend the opportunity for children to encounter familiar and meaningful situations beyond the home corner by creating another imaginative play area. This could be a launderette, a supermarket, a baby clinic, a garage or any one of a host of other possibilities. A wonderful example of doing this is given by **Hall and Robinson** (1995) where they describe how a teacher took her class to visit a local garage and then set up a garage in the classroom. The teacher was particularly interested in developing children's writing skills and the children embarked on a number of exciting and unusual writing acts where they did things like filling in forms for planning permission, writing letters, designing posters, etc. Drawing from the meaningful context of the garage the children were able to explore the many different purposes for which people write in a way that made sense to them.

Let us pause now and summarise what has been covered so far:

- Children need a range of interesting and challenging objects and situations in which to play and learn.
- Children will learn best when the situations they find make sense to them and allow them to draw on what they already know and can do.
- The way in which resources are organised and labelled can encourage children to develop independence and make valid choices.

- The resources should reflect both the cultures and languages of the children in the group.

PLANNING YOUR ACTIVITIES

In many nurseries and playgroups the adults tend to offer the basic things like sand and water, construction and home corner play each day, together with a number of 'table-top' activities – things like jigsaw puzzles, cutting and sticking and junk modelling. This type of planning reflects planning without considering the individual needs of the children and sometimes means that the children become fixed in their play and may become bored and trouble-some. Let us refer back to some of what we covered in the first chapter and remind ourselves of what **Vygotsky** called the 'Zone of Proximal Develop-ment'. He said that what children can do with help is far more than they can do unaided. The implication of this is that we need to be aware of what the child can do alone and then help the child to make the next leap in learning.

You cannot, of course, closely study each of 30 children every day to assess their present level and think of what you can do to take each child's learning forward. This would be a physical and intellectual impossibility. What you can do, however, is to select a number of children to observe closely each day or even to observe one area of your room and take note of how the children play and learn in that area.

Here are two examples to illustrate ways of doing this:

At the end of each day the staff gather together for a brief, but focused summary of the day's events. In this playgroup each staff member is a keyworker for a number of children and it is these children they focus on. Of course they may not focus on each of these children every day, but they keep careful notes to ensure that no child is forgotten or overlooked.

Maria, a parent volunteer, comments that Jordan has been unsettled and weepy and suggests that it may be the presence of the new baby that is upsetting her. The group decided that they will set up a baby clinic in the home corner area and spend a few minutes discussing what materials and equipment they will need and how they will gather this together.

The group leader, Alicia, says she thinks that four-year-old Hamish is on the verge of reading. She observed him retelling the story of 'Not Now Bernard' and actually pointing to the words as he did so. She volunteers to take a group of the older children (those who are interested and hopefully including Hamish) to make a 'Big Book' version of the story. The children can do the illustrations and she will model the writing by doing it in front of them. She can invite individual children to guess what letter a word starts with or to write words she knows they can write.

Paulette thinks that three-year-old Sukvinder is including Urdu symbols in her 'writing'. She suggests inviting Sukvinder's mother in to sit in the writing corner and maybe write a letter in Urdu. She will make sure that there is writing paper, envelopes and stamps in the writing area.

Alicia says that four-year-old Darren is very interested in circles. He has been drawing them, making circular movements out in the garden and including circles in all his attempts at writing. She wants to put out a lot of circular shapes in the junk modelling area and observe what Darren does with these.

You will see that in this example the adults have been paying close attention to the children in order to decide how to help them in their learning. In the next example you will find the staff focusing more on what they have provided and using this as the basis for planning:

In this nursery each member of staff takes responsibility for setting up a number of activities and then spends time in them observing the children at play.

Lettie says that she had put a number of plastic containers in the water tray. 'Some of the children were filling them up with water and then pushing them to the bottom of the water tray to try and make them sink. I'm going to put the same containers in the water tomorrow, but I'm also going to include some stones. I want to see if the children try putting the stones in the containers and see what happens.'

Julian says that he read a group of children 'The Jolly Postman' and that they were really interested in the letters. He is going to put writing paper and envelopes out in the writing area and is going to rescue the postbox they had around at Christmas time. The nursery head suggests that he might like to base himself in the writing area and be seen by the children actually writing a letter himself.

Natasha has been observing the home corner and says that she feels that the children are really stuck in their play. They seem to act out the same sequences every day. 'I am going to bring in something new to see if that changes the play' she says. 'Why don't you set up the home corner in the nursery by putting an old toaster on the table together with some tools from the woodwork area?' suggests the nursery head.

A number of important points have been raised by these examples. In the first place, it is clear that in order to plan for learning and development, you have to pay close attention to what children are doing and what they are interested in. In the second place, it is worth remembering that children do need long periods of time in order to get deeply involved in what they are doing. If you divide up your day into short periods of 'work' and 'play' you make this impossible. Further, children sometimes need to explore something not just over one day, but over several. In the second example you will have noticed that Lettie was not going to put something completely different in the water on the following day. She was going to let the children continue their exploration of whether or not the plastic containers would sink or not, but she was going to add something new to the existing activity. Now this is a vital point for all nursery workers. Where children are interested in exploring something, adding something new or even taking something away from the activity will offer the children an intellectual challenge and encourage them to further their explorations.

Can you think of how the addition of stones to the water tray would offer the children a cognitive challenge? Or would you prefer to put completely different things in the water the next day?

Lettie, possibly without knowing it, is operating the theory of 'Match' devised by **McVicker Hunt**. He believed that children will be assisted in their learning when they are offered something new in a situation, but he emphasised that the gap between the old and the new must be neither too big nor too small. Where the gap between what the child is exploring and the new situation is too big, children are not able to make the cognitive leap involved. Where the gap is too small, there is no intellectual challenge and the children will not be learning. Lettie believed that the children were exploring whether or not the containers, filled with water, would sink. By offering them stones to put inside the containers she was helping them realise something about weight and buoyancy. Had she decided to remove the plastic containers and put just some stones in the water she would not have allowed the children to make the link between what they had been doing (filling the containers) and the new activity. The theory of 'Match' is a very useful one for nursery workers and is certainly worth bearing in mind when planning activities.

You will see the link between the theory of 'Match' and the work of Vygotsky. The introduction of the novel object or activity helps the child move from where he or she is now to a higher plane of learning and understanding.

Often, when workers are asked why they have provided an activity for children – something like 'cutting and sticking' for example – they respond by saying things like 'Well, the children really love it'.

26

In light of what you have read so far do you think that this is an appropriate or adequate response?

Children like all sorts of things. They like eating sweets and drinking Coca Cola and watching TV. This does not mean that these things are good for them. As nursery workers our goals must be to enhance children's learning and development and all activities should be planned with some valid learning goal in mind. If you are planning a cutting and sticking activity your reason might be to help develop children's use of fine tools. When you plan your activities on the basis of what you have observed about the children you will almost inevitably have to have a learning goal in mind.

Let us now summarise this section:

- Activities need to be planned to meet the learning needs of children.
- Adults need to pay careful attention to what children are doing in order to take their learning forward.
- Workers need to work as a team in order to share their observations and plan together. This is both efficient and informative. Sharing information and planning together brings about an element of continuity and a sense of shared values.
- Introducing something new (either by bringing in a novel object or by removing something) can take learning forward as long as the gap between the old and the new is carefully matched.
- Children need extended periods of time in which to explore. This allows them to follow their own interests and solve the problems they set themselves in their play.
- The best planning does not mean offering something different every day. Children may need to do the same things over and over again.

INTERVENING AND INTERACTING

It is a sunny Monday morning and all the children are out in the garden area. Some are playing in the sandpit, some are on the climbing frames, some are racing round on bikes and trikes. The adult who is on 'duty' is sitting on a chair where she has a good view of all the activities. She is drinking a cup of tea and, every so often, yells a warning. Occasionally children come over to her to be comforted or to ask for something. When asked what her role is, she confidently replies that she is there in order to ensure that the children play safely. Her role is that of supervisor.

It is obvious that children's safety must be a prime concern and workers must do everything they can to ensure this. But since nurseries are about learning and development the role of the adult is much more important than merely supervision. It is about more than ensuring that you have provided a stimulating and challenging environment with many meaningful activities which you have planned according to what you have observed about children's existing knowledge and current interests.

From birth children are involved in interactive acts with adults and others. **Wells** (1986) believes that children are impelled to interact, especially through speech, because of their urge to communicate their desires and needs more explicitly. **Maxwell** (1996) believes that this urge extends to a need to be close, to experience warmth and acceptance.

For Wells interaction is like the act of throwing a ball to a small child:

> 'First ensure the child is ready with arms cupped to catch the ball, throw gently and accurately so that it lands squarely in the child's arms. When it is the child's turn to throw, the adult must be prepared to run wherever the ball goes.'

You will recognise in this example just how much responsibility for an effective interaction rests with the adult as the more experienced partner in the reciprocal exchange. Wells goes on to say:

> '. . . if the adult and child are to succeed in elaborating a shared meaning over a number of turns the adult has to make the effort to understand the child's intended meaning and to extend it in terms that the child can understand.'

This is the essence of effective interaction. Let us try and draw out the meaning more clearly. By 'shared meaning' Wells is talking about both parties – adult and child – paying attention to the same thing. The adult has to pay close attention to what it is the child is exploring in order that his or her interaction with the child can be focused on that. Adult sometimes have their own agenda in mind and when working with a child take the opportunity to teach the child something – the names of colours, numbers, shapes for example. But the child may be paying attention to something much more complex and if the adult is wrong in her guess about the child's focus of attention the interaction breaks down.

Here are some examples. In each case say first what you believe the child is paying attention to and then suggest what you might do or say. Do remember that there are no right or wrong answers.

> Jonas has been playing in the construction area every day for well over a week. Each time he constructs something he pays a great deal of attention to ensuring that his construction is symmetrical.

What might you say to him? And what might you introduce next into the construction area?

You notice that Rehana has taken a long strip of paper from the writing area and has gone over to the children's coat pegs and is laboriously copying each child's name in a list on this piece of paper.

What might you say to her? And what might you do next to foster her development in this area?

You have been doing some number songs with a group of children and you notice that three-year-old Bernie knows all the words and, what is more, uses her fingers when she is counting down.

What might you say to her? And what activities might you offer her next?

How did you get on with doing this? You might like to compare your responses with some gathered from workers in the area.

In the case of Jonas and his symmetrical buildings, one nursery worker said 'I would certainly use the word "symmetrical" in my response. I would say something like "My goodness, Jonas. Every time you make something it is the same on both sides. We call that symmetrical". I might then bring a mirror into the construction area and see what he makes of that. Or I could put out some folded paper and see if he is interested in something like "blot" paintings.'

In the case of Rehana making a list of names one nursery nurse said 'I would assume (perhaps wrongly) that Rehana was making a register. She sees us walking round each morning with a register, ticking off names. So, assuming she is drawing on this experience, I might try and just put in words what I think she is doing. I'd say "You're making a register, Rehana, just like the one I use in the mornings to check that the children are here." By doing this I would validate what she is doing and help her become conscious of what she already knows. If I noticed that she could actually recognise some of the names (and I am pretty sure she could) I might get her to help me check the register the next day. Or I could put out an empty register book and see what she does with that. In the longer term I would perhaps make a book for her in which we could include the names she recognises – like a song the children know: something like "Poor Jenny sits a weeping".'

In the case of three-year-old Bernie and her knowledge of numbers one playgroup worker said 'I would comment on what she already knows, perhaps by saying something like "You know all the words of the songs, Bernie, and you are using your fingers to count down. That's what I do, isn't it? And I sometimes use the children as well." I just want to draw her attention to her achievements. I would carry on doing number songs and maybe make her a book of one of them. She could help by doing the drawings or by sticking things in.'

If you think about how you interact with other people – your friends or colleagues or family – you will realise that all of your interactions involve relating *about* something. It may be about who is going to set up the garden equipment in the morning or about what film you are going to see or about who is collecting the children from school. **Bruner**'s research in 1980 showed that most of the interactions between teachers and children in schools focused on managerial issues and were primarily concerned with teachers responding to children's achievements with comments like 'good boy!' or 'well done!' Bruner suggests that those involved with children would do better to try and tune into what children are doing in more supportive ways. With older children interactions might involve discussing with children aspects of the task in which they have been involved. Whatever the interaction, the response of the adult gives the child some idea of the adult's views of the child, of learning, of the world. In other words interactions are about more than the child's behaviour or performance: they are part of the process of exchanging views and sharing meanings.

Let us now summarise what has been said in this section:

- Children learn through interaction with more experienced learners – either older children or adults.
- Interaction involves the sharing of meaning and requires the adult to pay close attention to the child's concerns in order that the child can be helped to make the next step.
- The role that adults play is complex, involving them in planning activities, talking to children, listening to children, observing children, thinking about what the children are doing, interacting.
- Adults should play a role that is more than merely supervising children's play.
- Children's learning can be scaffolded by the adult reflecting back to the child what the child already knows and can do. This helps the child become conscious of his or her own achievements.

It is clear that the role of the adult in supporting and extending children's learning is a complex one. Adults working with young children need to be knowledgable about how young children learn best and to be sensitive in their interactions with both children and their carers. A recent trend in some countries of calling all those who work with young children 'facilitators' is concerning. The use of this term implies that the role is limited to facilitating learning, and as we have seen in this chapter it is about much more than that. As an adult working with young children you will often be facilitating their learning, but you will also be planning for it, monitoring it, intervening in it to take learning forward. You will be listening, watching, considering, taking notes and making decisions based on your own knowledge of child development and of individual children. The vital role of the adult will be returned to time and again throughout this book.

REFERENCES

Bruner, J., *Under Five in Britain*, Grant McIntyre, 1980.

Hall, N. and Robinson, A., *Exploring Writing and Play in the Early Years*, David Fulton Publishers, 1995.

Maxwell, S., 'Meaningful Interaction' in Robson, S. and Smedley, S. (eds) *Education in Early Childhood*, David Fulton Publishers, 1996.

Wells, G., *The Meaning Makers*, Hodder and Stoughton, 1986.

3

THE EARLY YEARS CURRICULUM

There is an increasing tendency throughout the developed world for planners to believe that the earlier young children start formal learning, the better the results will be. From what you have read in Chapter 1 of this book you will know that the way in which young children learn is different from the way in which older children or adults learn. You will remember the work of **Lillian Katz** and **David Elkind** and their findings that children introduced to formal learning at too young an age may actually suffer long-term damage to their desire to be independent, to solve problems, to think for themselves and to carry on being curious.

Experts in the field of early childhood education have pleaded with government and planners to bear this in mind. In 1992 members of the Early Years Curriculum Group published a pamphlet entitled 'First Things First: Educating Your Children'. The pamphlet was written as a guide for parents and governors and serves as a reminder of some of the things we need to remember when developing a curriculum for young children. They summarise their views in a set of twelve principles which they believe are fundamental to good early years practice. We will examine some of these principles here.

1. Early childhood is the foundation on which children build the rest of their lives. It is important and valid in itself and should not be seen as the preparation for the next stage of life or of learning

This may seem obvious, but do remember how much pressure nursery workers are under to prepare children for Key Stage 1 of the National Curriculum in England and Wales. In many nursery classes attached to schools – which many of our four year olds attend – children are already regarded as working towards this. The implication of this is that children are being asked to engage in tasks which are often decontextualised (that is where the meaning is not clear to the child or embedded in the task) and too abstract for young children to cope with.

2. Children develop emotionally, socially, intellectually, morally, physically, spiritually and linguistically and they develop at different rates. All aspects of development are equally important and always interwoven

When you consider the development of the human infant it becomes clear that one aspect of development has clear implications for other aspects. Think of what happens when an infant is first able to sit upright. This is usually described as a physical 'milestone', but think of how this affects what the child can see, explore with his or her hands and discover about the world. Think of how the child's ability to sit unaided affects the child's social interactions. Development and learning in the early years cannot be separated out into categories. When a child begins to understand the symbolic function this is an intellectual 'milestone', if you like, but it comes about through the physical and sensory exploration of the world; it impacts on the child's play and relationships and has implications for all aspects of learning.

3. Young children learn from everything that happens to them and do not separate their learning into subjects

We can describe the National Curriculum as a syllabus, laying down what all children throughout the country should learn in different subject areas. A curriculum for young children implies much more than this. Since young children learn from everything that happens to them the curriculum involves all the learning activities they encounter, all the relationships they develop, all the social rules they are introduced to and all the routines of the day. Where young children are involved in the lunch time routines, for example, by helping to lay the table, talk to their friends and help clear up they have opportunities to explore number (one knife, one fork for each child, for example), social rules (passing the peas, sharing out the fruit) and, through talk, may explore past and future, ideas in their heads or anything else they choose to talk about. It is clear that the routines of the day and the ethos of the nursery or playgroup will have as much impact on children's learning as the more formal curriculum.

4. Young children learn by doing rather than by being told

A great deal of what happens in formal schooling involves instruction. Children as young as four are expected to sit quietly whilst they receive instructions or are given information. The evidence from research is clear. The younger the child the more opportunity he or she should have to be actively doing in order to actively make sense of any activity.

5. Children learn most effectively when they are actively involved and interested in what they are doing

Let us use an example to illustrate this point. The example refers to four-year-old Sacha who is in the reception class of his local school:

> Each morning Sacha is required to find his name card and to trace his name. When he has done that he is directed to the first activity of the day. The teacher reports that Sacha struggles to trace his name, which surprises his mother who has seen Sacha write his name and the names of his family and friends in the writing he chooses to do at home. When she tells the teacher this the information is received with a knowing smile which leads Sacha's mother to feel that she is being labelled as pushy. She resolves to say no more about what she believes that Sacha can do.

6. Children need time and space to produce work of quality and depth

We have touched on this in earlier chapters and seen how, when children are given long, uninterrupted periods of time in which to follow their own interests they can get involved for long periods of time and with intense concentration. The school day is often broken up into small units of time so that the subjects can be followed and things like PE and assembly and swimming and library can be fitted in. In the best nursery practice children have the whole morning and/or the whole afternoon in which they move from chosen activity to chosen activity or remain deeply engrossed in what they are doing. In such settings the routines of the day are regarded as part of the curriculum and children are involved in clearing up, in setting the tables and all other routines.

7. What children can do rather than what they cannot yet do should be the starting point for their learning

We have seen how **Piaget**'s focus on what children could not yet do in the stages of development he identified is of little help to those trying to plan for learning and development. Through close observation of the child at play workers gain a clear understanding of what the child can already do and this provides a sound starting point for all further learning. Since children are learning all the time, close observation needs to be an ongoing process. **Glenda Bissex** (1980) kept a record of her son Paul's development as a reader and writer. Her book makes fascinating reading and throws some powerful insights on the learning of young children. But she also raises some serious and troubling questions about what happens to learning once children start school. She asserts that, often, children learn not because of their teachers but despite them. She tries to encourage all educators to listen to children, to watch them and to try and understand what they are doing. She suggests that, rather than pushing children too fast, sometimes it is worth just watching and waiting in order to both support and extend learning. She says:

> 'We speak of starting with a child "where he is at", which in one sense is not to assert an educational desideratum but an inescapable fact: there is no other place the child can start from. There are only other places the teacher can start from.'

8. Playing and talking are the main ways in which young children learn

In the first chapter we examined theories of learning and saw how many theorists and researchers gave prominence to play and to language. You will remember that, in play, children are in charge of their own learning. They choose what to do and how to solve the problems they encounter. They cannot fail.

But what about talk? Why is it important to learning? Children are born with a powerful need to communicate. Research has shown that all children from all types of homes and speaking any of the world's languages acquire language which is useful for describing the world, solving problems, reflecting back and predicting into the future. Talk is the first form of language that children develop and this leads to the development of both reading and writing. When we listen to children talking we can gain a clearer understanding of what they already know both about language itself and about the world they inhabit. In addition to that we have seen how the spoken language used by adults can help children reflect on what they have achieved. You may be surprised to learn that there are some reception classes where children are expected to complete their 'work' in silence.

These are only some of the principles which are regarded as being fundamental to good early years practice. You may have a set of principles yourself. But these give us a starting point for looking at some examples of good early years practice.

Nursery provision in Emilia Romagna, Italy

In the wealthy area of Northern Italy the provision of high-quality child care and education has been a priority of all the local people since the end of the Second World War. Led by an idealist and educationalist, **Loris Malaguzzi**, local people obtained the resources and the support to establish a number of nurseries which are still the envy of the developed world. So much so that the number of visitors to these nurseries has had to be limited in recent years.

There are a number of features that make the provision special. Firstly, parents and other people in the local community are involved in the management of these nurseries and their words are listened to. Secondly, everything that happens is documented. Careful records are kept of every aspect of the work and these are analysed in order that successful things can be replicated and unsuccessful things dropped. All the nurseries are in purpose-built facilities and the architects and planners have to take account of the social, emotional and educational needs of the children and workers when designing the building and the equipment to go in it. Staff have good working conditions and an ongoing programme of in-service training.

Most impressive, however, is the quality of the work of the children. Visitors are often stunned by the intensity of the children's concentration as they draw and paint, use the computers, design and construct, make and send messages to one another and explore the physical space. The philosophy of the nurseries is that childhood is important in its own right and that children should encounter a range of meaningful experiences and activities in order that they become able to represent and re-represent what they have seen and heard and learned.

Here is an example to illustrate this:

In a nursery in Modena a project developed around the theme of lions. In Modena the cathedral, set in a magnificent square, has stone lions outside it. All the families of Modena use the square as a meeting place and all the children regard the lions as familiar. The staff took a group of children to visit the lions. The children took with them clipboards and pencils and they were invited to draw the lions if they wanted to. Back at the nursery a host of other activities were on offer. Some children drew the lions in pencil and then made large and brilliantly coloured paintings. Some made giant lions out of large cardboard boxes and junk materials. Some dressed up as lions and made up stories or dances. Some made lions out of clay, using tools skilfully and appropriately. In this way the children were able to represent their ideas and feelings about the lions in a range of ways. You will remember how learning involves the establishment of connections between brain cells. In this example each time a representation was made (a drawing or a model or a dance or a poem) another set of connections was established.

In another nursery in the same region the teachers (all workers are given the title of teacher) were concerned that children's links with the nursery might be damaged over the long summer holiday. So they gave each child a box and invited the children to put anything in the box they chose to remind them of the summer. The children were asked to bring the filled boxes back to the nursery when term resumed. One little girl had, in her box, a bus ticket. Through discussion, the staff discovered that it was the ticket she had used to go and visit her grandparents who lived at the seaside. When she was asked what she had seen at the seaside she surprised the adults by saying she had seen 'arms and legs'. They had been expecting her to say 'buckets and spades' or 'ice creams'. As sensitive and exploring teachers the adults explored further and discovered that the seaside town the little girl had visited was situated on a steep hillside and, in order to get to the beach, she had to walk down steep streets. Put yourself in the position of a four year old and you will realise that in doing this you are, indeed, surrounded by a forest of arms and legs. The staff started talking to the children about what was meant by the word 'crowd' and they discovered that most of the children thought that a crowd meant a group of people all going in the same direction.

Stop at this point and consider what you might have done to take the children's understanding of a crowd further.

Here is what the staff at the nursery above did. They first took the children out into the square so that they could be part of a crowd and notice that not all the people were going in the same direction. They then suggested that the children draw one another – from the front, from the back and in profile. They then enlarged some of the drawings and shrunk others using the photocopier. The final versions were coloured in by the children, cut out and mounted on card so that they would stand upright. The resulting collection of images were placed upright in a large box so that the children had a symbolic representation of a crowd.

The work of these Italian nursery schools is underpinned by a clear philosophy which embraces many of the points outlined in the principles for high-quality early learning. The type of curriculum that emerges from this is one that can be described as developmental. Such a curriculum takes as its starting point a dynamic view of development. This recognises that human development changes over time and with experience so that the ways in which young children learn are recognised as different from the ways in which older children and adults learn. Such a dynamic view also recognises the impact of what is called 'delayed impact' which refers to the ways in which early experience may affect later functioning, particularly with regard to the development of self-esteem, social development, feelings and dispositions. The third aspect of a developmental viewpoint is the long-term cumulative effect of frequent experiences. This implies that something that happens to a young child once or twice may be beneficial in the short term, but repeated exposure over a long period of time may have damaging effects.

These are quite difficult ideas to grasp but they are important to those of us concerned with promoting early learning and development. Malaguzzi (personal communication, 1992) said that he knew that once children started school they would be exposed to what he described as tedious and meaningless tasks – things like colouring in, joining the dots, tracing their names, completing jigsaw puzzles. He urged us:

> 'Look around you at the remarkable creative and original things the children can do and then think about how the school teachers, by ignoring all that children have already done and achieved by the time they start school, make the children feel stupid and ignorant and give them things that offer no intellectual challenge. The teachers in schools keep telling us that we don't "teach" the children properly. By that they mean that we don't train them to do meaningless things. I say to them "We give our children a sense of their own identity, opportunities to express their thoughts and ideas through some of the hundred languages at their disposal (writing, drawing, building, designing, acting, dancing, singing) and we believe that we lay a foundation which will allow the children to get through their schooling with their attitude to learning and discovery undamaged. That is our job." I say to them "Maybe you should learn from us and not expect us to prepare the children for years of tedium and boredom."'

Contrast this developmental approach with an example offered by **Lillian Katz**. In an American preschool a group of four year olds were engaged in what Katz describes as the 'calendar ritual'. Katz describes what happened as follows:

> 'With the children seated on the floor facing a large calendar showing the month of February, the teacher asks them what day it is today. They call out the days of the week in what appears to be random fashion, and by chance none offers the correct answer; which is Thursday. The teacher then asks, "What day was it yesterday?" The same array of guesses is offered, which fortunately includes Wednesday. She responds "That's right! So what day is it today?" Eventually she coaxes them into agreeing on the correct answer.
> When she asks next for the date (the 19th) no one replies. She then asks one of the children to come forward and write the correct numbers in the appropriate empty box on the calendar. When he hesitates, she suggests that he look at the number for yesterday.

Unfortunately, he looks in the box above rather than to the left of the empty one. Because it contains the number 12, the child says 13. Pointing out that he has looked "the wrong way" the teacher asks, "What comes after 18?" She thereby persuades him to agree on the date, which he manages to write almost legibly in the box . . .'

Katz points out that the children involved were far too young to understand the concept of the date, but because they are eager to please the teacher they behave with great courtesy, attempting to produce the answer that will satisfy her. Katz goes on to say that if something like this happened to young children once or twice in the early years it would probably have no deleterious effect. But in many preschool settings in the United States and in many reception classes in schools this type of decontextualised activity happens with monotonous regularity, day in and day out. As we have said before, young children will learn from all experiences and they may learn undesirable as well as desirable things. For Katz, then, the developmental question is not so much what children can do or even how they learn. The question is what should they do that will best help their learning and development in the long term. Katz urges that those working with young children pay attention not only to what is known about how young children learn, but also take heed of the effects of the long-term cumulative effects of the experiences they encounter.

For us, then, the message is that the curriculum is not only about what children should learn, but crucially how they should learn. What we, the adults, do is crucial to their learning and development in the long term.

ONE WAY OR MANY?

Most of the research and theory quoted here has come from a Western perspective. It is important to remember that the users of our preschool services come from a range of backgrounds, with varying expectations and differing values. In their book *Preschool in Three Cultures*, **Tobin**, **Wu** and **Davidson** examine an American preschool, a Japanese preschool and a Chinese preschool and their findings provide much food for thought.

In American preschools the pursuit of happiness is often one of the explicit goals, whereas Chinese preschools are regarded as places of serious learning where, if the children are happy as they learn, so much the better, but happiness is a by-product and not a goal. The Japanese preschools aim to produce children who are childlike and this means that they will often be happy but may also be angry, frustrated, lonely or selfish. The outcome of this is that Japanese children are encouraged to learn through play in a loosely planned environment where the adults stay on the fringes of children's play and do not intervene in order to support and extend learning.

It is obvious, too, that preschools in affluent societies will be better resourced and equipped than those in poorer countries. American preschools provide children with an overwhelming amount of toys, books, miniature versions of adult things (like irons and hoovers), outdoor equipment, and so on. On the walls are children's drawings and images of 'happy' things – like cartoon characters, animals dressed like people and nursery rhymes. The question arises as to whether such an abundance of equipment is necessary for learning and development. If the answer to this question is yes, ill-equipped playgroups will feel that they have no chance to compete with their better-equipped counterparts. A Japanese preschool teacher commented as follows:

> 'We don't have a make-believe corner, but children in our school play lots of imaginary games. They play house and store and fireman. You don't need costumes and plastic dishes to play house. You don't need a fireman's hat to pretend you're a fireman. I don't think that children need all of those special things to play. Don't teachers in America believe children have imagination?'
> (Tobin, Wu and Davidson, 1989)

This may be consoling for you if you are struggling to gather together all the materials and resources you see so glossily displayed in educational catalogues. It is worth bearing in mind that more than half the world's children learn and play using natural, found and real materials.

Although all parents recognise that children play and through their play learn, many of them fall into the trap of believing that once children start in the nursery or school they should put playing away and start to 'learn for real'. One of the most difficult things workers have to do is to explain to parents why play is important. Workers can only do that if they themselves understand this and understand how play is different from work.

In 1996 the Curriculum and Assessment Authority for Wales published a consultation document on their proposal to introduce their 'Desirable Outcomes for Children's Learning Before Compulsory School Age'. In this they talk in some detail about the early years curriculum, reminding readers that it is about the child and that it is concerned not only with content but also with the context of learning. In other words, the process is just as important as the product or outcome. This is a vital point and one to which we will return again and again when we turn our attention to the final version of the 'Desirable Outcomes for Children's Learning on Entering Compulsory Education'.

The Welsh document goes on to talk in some detail about the importance of play. It is worth quoting here what they say:

> 'Children's play is a very serious business indeed. It needs concentrated attention. It is all about perseverance, attending to detail,

learning and concentrating – characteristics usually associated with work. Play is work and work is play for the young child. Play is not only crucial to the way children become self-aware and the way in which they learn the rules of social behaviour, it is also fundamental to intellectual development.

Young children learn most effectively when they are actively involved in first hand experiences. Young children's learning is a hands-on business. An education service for young children is about the child. It is about adults understanding, inspiring and challenging the child's talent to learn.

Adult involvement in children's play is of vital importance. Good early years educators are there to help children, to guide their play, to offer choices when the playing flags, to challenge children with care and sensitivity, to encourage them and to move their learning along.'

The document goes on to look at what it calls 'the principle of appropriateness'. By this they are adopting the developmental approach described earlier. They point out that young children vary in rates of growth and development. You will have come across four year olds who look like six year olds and four year olds who look like two year olds. The same variation is true of intellectual development. A curriculum designed for young children must acknowledge this fact and those working with young children need to understand that we cannot say that all four year olds should be able to write their names, for example. What we can say is that most four year olds given the opportunity will be able to write their names, recognising that there will be some children who will not learn to write their names until they are five or six. This does not necessarily indicate that these children are 'slow learners': rather it suggest that these children have not yet developed an interest in learning to write their names. Their concerns lie elsewhere.

Let us now pause and review what has been said so far with regard to an early years curriculum before we look in some detail at the 'Desirable Outcomes for Children's Learning on Entering Compulsory Education'.

- An early years curriculum is about more than content: it is about the context in which learning takes place. This means that the process is just as important as the outcomes.
- An early years curriculum is about the child. Childhood should be regarded as important in its own right and not seen as preparation for the next stage or phase.
- The views of parents and users are important and should be considered when developing the curriculum.
- Workers need to understand the importance of play for learning and be able to explain this clearly to parents.

- Resources should be there to support learning. Learning is possible even when resources are limited.
- Young children vary enormously in their rates of development and this should be recognised and acknowledged by workers.
- Workers need to remember that young children learn best by doing rather than by being told and that language is essential for learning.
- Children need time and space in order to pursue their concerns in depth. The day should not be broken down into small segments of time and the routines of the day should be seen as opportunities to extend learning.

'Desirable Outcomes for Children's Learning on Entering Compulsory Education'

The previous Conservative Government introduced the Nursery Education Voucher Scheme and set out the proposals in two related documents. In 'The Next Steps' the government described how the new nursery vouchers for all four year olds would work, and in the 'Desirable Outcomes' it laid out the criteria for assessing children's attainment when they reach the age of compulsory schooling – that is in the term after the child's fifth birthday. The new Labour Government has abolished nursery vouchers but has made a commitment to fund through the local authorities places for all four year olds. The goals for children's learning set out in the 'Desirable Outcomes' document will still be relevant and these goals have now also been incorporated into the OFSTED inspection framework used for inspecting nursery classes and nursery schools. Therefore we will look in some detail at what these desirable outcomes are and what they mean for practitioners.

Here is what is said in the introduction to the document:

> 'The desirable outcomes are goals for learning for children by the time they enter compulsory education. They emphasise early literacy, numeracy and the development of personal and social skills and contribute to children's knowledge, understanding and skills in other areas. Presented as six areas of learning, they provide a foundation for later achievement.'

Although the document does go on to refer to the fact that children will progress at different rates, it clearly regards these six areas of learning as constituting the curriculum. You will remember that, earlier in this chapter, we talked about how high-quality early years education is as much about the process as it is about the product – the outcomes, in this case. You will also remember that a good early years curriculum refers to all the experiences a child encounters and not only to acquiring a body of knowledge and a repertoire of skills. One last point: you might like to ask yourself whether the approach here reflects a view of childhood as important in itself or sees it merely as a preparation for the next stage – that is for Key Stage 1.

The six areas of learning identified in the document are as follows.

Personal and Social Development   The Outcomes focus on how the child is learning to work, play and cooperate with others and to function in a wider group than that of the family. The Outcomes look at the development of personal values and an understanding of self and others.

Language and Literacy   The Outcomes look at aspects of the development of language and the foundations of literacy. They focus on children's competence in English but do allow for this to be achieved through support for the child's first language(s). The Outcomes emphasise the child's developing competence in speaking and listening, reading and writing.

Mathematics   The Outcomes address various areas of mathematical understanding but place most emphasis on numeracy. They focus on achievement through practical activities and on helping children develop the language of mathematics.

Knowledge and Understanding of the World   The Outcomes focus on children's developing knowledge and understanding of their environment, of other people and of features of the natural and the man-made world. They include the traditional subject areas of history, geography, science and technology.

Physical Development   The Outcomes focus on children's developing physical skills, both gross and fine, and include mobility, awareness of space and ability to use fine tools. Included is a concern for developing attitudes towards a healthy and active way of life.

Creative Development   The Outcomes here focus on children's abilities to develop their imagination and express their ideas and feelings in creative ways and in order to communicate.

Although the document clearly outlines what it is that children should experience before they start formal schooling it does not tell us how they should be 'taught'. It does identify some common features of good practice and we will examine these here to see if they fit with some of the things we have already read.

1.   Children learn best if they feel secure and confident and they will feel secure and confident when they are offered a sense of achievement through the learning they encounter both at home and in their preschool settings.

2. All settings should have a statement of their aims, objectives and the content of their curriculum which they share with parents or carers. In this statement should be information about how children's progress is assessed and how information about their progress will be passed on to parents and to the schools to which the children will go.

3. There should be a good relationship between the setting and other professionals in the area – health clinics, health visitors, child-minders and local schools.

4. Children should be able to participate in a range of activities which allow them to follow their own interests and build on their previous knowledge and experience. Through this children will develop their physical, intellectual, social and emotional skills.

5. Children should be encouraged to think and talk about their learning in order to develop self-control and independence. They should be allowed long lengths of time in order to get deeply involved in sustained activity. There should be an emphasis on first-hand experience, on giving clear explanations, on appropriate adult intervention and on using play and talk as media for learning.

6. Children's progress should be assessed through observation. Notes on their progress should be recorded and shared with parents. Workers should be alert to children's particular needs and should seek early identification of and support for any special needs.

7. The physical environment should support learning by offering appropriate space, facilities and equipment and should be organised with regard to the health and safety of all the users.

8. Children's progress will be enhanced when the adults working with them are appropriately trained and aware of how children learn best. Settings are regarded as being responsible for identifying and meeting the training needs of staff.

SUMMING IT UP

The 'Desirable Outcomes' document then provides settings with the outline of a curriculum in the sense of recommending the areas of learning which should be provided for children, indoors and out. It does not prescribe how such activities should be provided, what sorts of intervention will best support learning or what training it is essential for the staff to have. These are left to the settings to decide.

The staff at Rainbow Playgroup set about deciding on their curriculum, the principles that would underpin it and their goals as follows:

> We are going to set up activities, indoors and out, which will allow children the following experiences:

- opportunities to develop motor skills;
- opportunities to use tools;
- opportunities to make plans;
- opportunities for speaking and listening;
- opportunities for reading and writing;
- opportunities for counting, for sorting, for matching, for one-to-one correspondence;
- opportunities for exploring space and shape;
- opportunities to explore pattern;
- opportunities to express ideas through drawing, painting, using clay and malleable materials, through music, through dance, through imaginative play;
- opportunities to understand the physical world through observing, making guesses, trying things out;
- opportunities to understand the world through going on visits, looking at images and artefacts, through books and stories, through reflecting the languages and cultures of our community;
- opportunities to develop social skills through role play, the routines of the day, through sharing and negotiating.

We will make sure that the activities we provide make human sense to the children so that they can see the purpose of the activities and build on their previous experience.

We will observe children regularly, keep notes on what we see and then share these with one another in an attempt to understand what each child is doing, where each child is. We will plan activities based on these assessments.

We will make our notes available to parents and invite them to tell us about the child at home. This will take some time to develop, but it is one of our goals for the coming year.

Zerrin is taking responsibility for Special Needs, so if we are worried about a child she will be our first port of call.

We are going to meet once a week after hours in order to improve our own skills. We have decided that our focus for this year will be on how we can support the children's learning through intervention. We are going to invite in some guest speakers to talk to us and have already started looking for books or videos to support us in doing this.

You can see from this plan just how many of the principles of high-quality early years education this group has taken on. They have planned a programme for themselves and for the children which is aimed at taking learning forward. In subsequent chapters we will return to this group and see how their plans are taking shape.

REFERENCES

Department for Education and Employment, 'The Next Steps', DfEE, 1996.

Early Years Curriculum Group, *First Things First*, Boon Printers, 1992.

Elkind, D., 'Formal Education and Early Childhood Education: An Essential Difference' in *Phi Delta Kappa*, May 1986.

Katz, L., 'What Should Young Children Be Doing?' in *American Educator*, Summer 1988.

Malaguzzi, L. with Gandini, L., 'History, Ideas and Basic Philosophy' in Edwards, C. *et al.* (eds) *The One Hundred Languages of Children*, Ablex Publishing Corporation, 1995.

School Curriculum and Assessment Authority, 'Desirable Outcomes for Children's Learning on Entering Compulsory Education', DfEE, 1996.

Tobin, J.J., Wu, D.Y.H. and Davidson, D.H., *Preschool in Three Cultures*, Yale University Press, 1989.

4

LIVING AND COMMUNICATING IN A SOCIAL WORLD

In this chapter we examine in detail what children are expected to know and do by the time they reach compulsory school age in two areas of learning: Personal and Social Development and Language and Literacy Development. More importantly we look at ways of promoting the development of the Desirable Outcomes in ways which fit in with what is known about how young children learn best.

PERSONAL AND SOCIAL DEVELOPMENT

Young children have been learning about themselves and others and about their place in the world since birth. By the time they have reached the age of four the majority of children clearly have a sense of their own identity, they know that they are unique. They have established relationships with other people – parents, carers, siblings, family members, friends and others. They can feed and dress themselves, use the toilet and make choices and decisions about what they want to do. They are curious and eager to learn as much as possible about the world they live in. They have developed some understanding that other people have feelings and emotions and can sometimes show concern and empathy for others. They have also started to work out something about how the social rules operate. **Judy Dunn** (1988) studied very young children at home in their family settings and demonstrated that, from an early age, children work out something about the feelings and the goals of others, the social rules and begin to understand other people's minds.

This is a considerable amount to have learned in a short space of time and it is important to remind ourselves that, since children learn from everything that happens to them, their social development has implications for their intellectual development, their language development and their physical development. All aspects of learning and development are interlinked.

The 'Desirable Outcomes' state that, by the age of five, most children should:

1. be confident, show appropriate self-respect and be able to establish
effective relationships with other children and with adults

For most children, in most settings, ensuring this should not be difficult. It is important to remember, however, that children are most likely to develop confidence and self-respect where they are shown respect in return. This means that children's first languages and their home cultures should be explicitly recognised and celebrated. Children are most likely to feel good about themselves when they are accepted and valued. Most of what children have learned when they start in any preschool setting has come from home. Where there is a clash between the values of home and those of the setting, children's confidence and self-esteem is damaged.

This raises an important and difficult question. How are workers expected to reconcile their values and their understanding of child development with the views and desires of parents? **Eve Gregory** (1995) graphically describes how the teacher of a Chinese child in Northampton was faced with this situation:

> 'Tony enters school smiling. . . . A month later, Tony's behaviour has undergone a complete change. His smile has disappeared, replaced, in Mrs G's words, by a "dead-pan look" which "you can't seem to get through to".'

In an effort to regain Tony's initial enthusiasm for school Mrs G visits the family at home, bringing with her an attractive dual-language picture/ storybook which she invites the family to share with him. Tony's grandfather refuses to accept the book, stating that Tony cannot have the book until he can read the words in it. Tony's grandfather goes on to show disgust at Tony's attempts to write his name in English – ToNy. In disgust, the grandfather states:

> '"This is from his English school. This is rubbish. . . . Look. He can't even write his name yet!".'

The teacher, Mrs G, has a clearly thought out philosophy about how young children learn and describes this philosophy as being 'child-centred'. Gregory goes on to say that Mrs G's plight highlights the position of many teachers and workers – and that is the tension between starting from where each child is and seeing each child as an individual and yet promoting an approach to learning and teaching which fits into currently accepted models of 'good practice'. The important point, Gregory believes, is that discontinuity between home and school or setting is more damaging to children's confidence and self-esteem – and hence to their learning and development – than the adoption of an accepted model of teaching. Workers need to listen to parents: they need to pay attention, to treat parents' views and experience with respect and to make sure that they are able to explain clearly why they are doing things. Discontinuity between home and school does not only apply to children who have languages other than English. In her book *Ways with Words* **Shirley Brice Heath** (1983) showed how in one community in America some children came to school with values which matched those of the school whilst others did not. All the children were competent learners, fluent speakers of their own languages and well aware of the social rules and mores of their communities. Yet once in school, those whose experience was different from that of the teachers and whose cultures were unfamiliar began to fail.

Young children move from playing on their own to playing alongside other children. As they get older they begin to interact in their play and, by the time children have reached the age of four, many of them will be engaged in what is known as 'cooperative play'. In such play children collaborate on a shared project or topic. In your setting you will want to ensure that there are opportunities for such play. Here is an example to illustrate this:

> The children have been to visit the local fire station. When they returned they helped the worker make a book about their visit, using photographs taken and their own drawings. On the following day the workers put out near the climbing frame a small ladder, some lengths of hose pipe and some plastic helmets. The children are engaged, over a long period of time, in playing 'fires'. As they play they negotiate roles 'You be the mum and I'll come up the ladder and rescue you'. They help one another by passing things, holding the ladder, sharing and communicating.

It is important to remember that, sometimes, even four year olds may resort to 'solitary play'. There is nothing wrong with this. You have only to think about yourself and how, sometimes, you want to do things alone to see that this is not a sign of immaturity.

2. work as part of a group and independently, are able to concentrate and persevere in their learning and to seek help where needed

We have already looked at children working as part of a group and independently. Children are most likely to concentrate and persevere in their learning when they are engaged in something they have chosen to do – that is, when they are playing.

Here are two examples. You decide which is most likely to promote the Desirable Outcome above.

The worker gathers a group of four year olds and asks them to join her at a table on which she has put out copies of a worksheet. She wants the children to learn the letter 'a' and on the worksheet are pictures of things the names of which start with this letter – apple, ant, alligator and so on. The children have to name the objects, say what letter they start with and colour them in. She notices that, although the children comply with her requests, she often has to bring them back to the task in hand. They are not deeply involved.

Rainbow Playgroup has set up a 'writing corner'. It has pens and pencils, a stapler, a hole punch, envelopes, writing paper, little booklets and blank forms. On the wall is an alphabet chart of the English alphabet, an alphabet chart in Bengali (the language spoken by some of the children) and examples of children's writing. There is a set of magnetic letters, an old typewriter and several alphabet books. Phuti and Tyrone spend more than an hour in this area. They write in the blank books, staple blank forms to the books, move the magnetic letters around to spell out their names and laugh together at some of the funny pictures in one of the alphabet books.

We have talked earlier about the complex role of the adult in any early years setting. One of the important things adults do is to let children know that they can ask for help. Often, once children start school, they become reluctant to ask for help because they get the message that only stupid children need help. This is not the case. We all need help sometimes and it is important the children know that asking for help is an appropriate and intelligent thing to do.

Here is an example to illustrate this:

> You will remember that, in Chapter 1, we looked at how Susan Bragg supported Louisa in the junk modelling area. Here are some of the comments and suggestions Susan made to indicate to Louisa that asking for help was an appropriate thing to do:
> 'These are left-handed scissors, Louisa. You are right-handed.'
> 'What do you think we can use to stick it, Louisa?'
> 'What about using an elastic band?'

3. are eager to explore new learning and show the ability to initiate ideas and to solve simple practical problems

We have seen that the human infant is born as if preprogrammed to make sense of the world. This innate curiosity is something that it is important to promote. **Lillian Katz** calls aspects of learning like curiosity 'dispositions' and has demonstrated how such dispositions can be damaged through too early exposure to formal learning. Children's curiosity is most likely to be promoted when they are able to follow their own concerns in a stimulating and challenging environment which offers first-hand experience, talk and appropriate adult intervention.

Here is an example given by **Mary Smith** (1995) to illustrate this:

> The children were interested in some bees in the centre garden. One boy wanted to know how honey was made. He suggested that they make some in the centre. Mary asked him how this could be done and he said that they needed to get together some flowers – daisies, buttercups and dandelions that were growing wild in the garden. He duly gathered these together and put them in a plastic tray. Daniel (aged 4.6) then said 'We have to pick out the pollen from the middle of each flower' and then spent a considerable amount of time doing this. When he was satisfied that he had got all the pollen he asked Mary to get him a cup and spoon. Daniel put the pollen in the cup and stirred it around a bit. After a while Mary asked him what was happening to the pollen. 'Nothing' he replied 'we have to add apple juice and then we will have honey'.

4. *demonstrate independence in selecting an activity or resources and in dressing and personal hygiene*

If your setting is organised in a way that fosters children's autonomy they will gain more and more experience of making their own choices, selecting the materials they want and in making decisions. The message, again, is that children should be encouraged to follow their own interests and should continue to learn through play.

5. *are sensitive to the needs and feelings of others and show respect for people of other cultures and beliefs*

Much of children's learning about feelings comes through their interactions with others and through the responses they receive from the adults around them. Lillian Katz (1994) says that the qualities we want to develop in children – things like caring for and about others, being honest and kind and accepting of difference, loving learning – are most likely to develop when children have exposure to adults and older children who display these qualities. She says:

> 'Children need relationships and experiences with adults who are willing to take a stand on what is worth doing, worth having,

worth knowing and worth caring about. This proposition seems to belabour the obvious. But in an age of increasing emphasis on pluralism, multiculturalism and community participation, professionals are increasingly hesitant and apologetic about their own values. It seems to me that such hesitancy to take a stand on what is worthwhile may cause us to give children unclear signals about what is worth knowing and doing and what is expected.'

6. take turns and share fairly, express their feelings and behave in appropriate ways, developing an understanding of what is right, what is wrong and why

One of the ways of assessing children's personal, social and emotional development is looking to see if they display a range of emotions and whether these emotions are appropriate.

Here are some examples to illustrate these points:

> Abby came to nursery very angry for a week or so. Before that she had seemed very settled, so we asked her carer if anything had changed at home. We were distressed to find that Abby's mother had been admitted to hospital and realised that the child was displaying emotions appropriate to her distress.

> Jordan is very withdrawn. At first we thought he was shy. He would not join in any activities, but sat in the book corner hugging a cuddly toy. We are still concerned, however, because he has now been here for three months and we have seen no sign of him coming out of this. We need to talk more to his parents.

In your setting you will want to ensure that children are encouraged to share and take turns. You will also want to help children come to understand what is right and what is wrong and to appreciate the reasons for this. Telling a child that he or she is 'being naughty' or putting the child in a 'cooling off chair', for example, is not likely to help the child develop an understanding of right and wrong. Judy Dunn (1988) gives some examples of parents helping children to appreciate right from wrong:

> 'In one example a child of under two kicks her sister accidentally. The younger child looks anxious and the mother, whilst comforting the older child, helps the younger one deal with her action by apologising to her sister and by saying "It was a mistake. She didn't mean to, darling. It was an accident".'

7. *treat living things, property and their environment with care and concern*

Children are most likely to develop these understandings when they are in an environment where things are properly cared for and living things – including children, parents, workers, cleaners, visitors – are treated with respect. If they see you, the adults, making sure that the toys and equipment are properly maintained and cared for they will learn to do the same thing. If there is a place for everything that is clear to the children they will help with clearing up and, as they do so, will be able to use their developing skills and knowledge about what belongs together, what belongs where and how things are best kept.

Here is an example to illustrate this:

> In a playgroup the staff became irritated at how careless the children were about things like putting paintbrushes away properly and replacing the lids on the felt pens. They decided to make caring for the materials a central theme of their work for a week or two. They took time to explain to the children that brushes stored with their bristles down will become misshapen and impossible to use and that felt pens will dry up without their lids on. Storing the brushes and replacing pen lids became part of the routines of the day and the staff were delighted to overhear a three year old tell an older child 'Don't put it like that! It goes all curly and then you can't paint properly with it. Do it like this!'

8. *respond to relevant cultural and religious events and show a range of feeling, such as wonder, joy or sorrow, in response to their experiences of the world*

All our children are growing up in a rich and multicultural world. It is vital that they encounter adults who enjoy the diversity of our society and show the languages, cultures and religions of the children equal respect. You may want to consider whether this is best done by celebrating the odd festival and occasionally offering some of the traditional foods to the children or whether it should be more deeply embedded in the everyday activities offered to the children.

Here is how one London teacher, **Birgit Voss** (1995), describes how she and her co-workers prepare for the coming term:

> 'I make a note of the different languages our little community will be using for the next four months: Gujerati, Bengali, Turkish, Urdu, Cantonese, Persian, Arabic, German and, of course, English. I check

these against our present resources. We have cassette story and video story tapes in all the languages but Cantonese. We have plenty of writing samples, newspapers and magazines in Chinese as we had some Chinese speaking children earlier. When we celebrated Chinese New Year – the Year of the Dog – we stocked up during a visit to the local Chinese supermarket. We also have appropriate clothes, fabrics and home base equipment, and lots of pictures. The parents seemed very open, friendly and cooperative during the home visit. I am sure they would love to make some story tapes, maybe sing some songs for us. Something to organise.'

Voss goes on to explain that the children in her nursery class learn from first-hand experience by building on what they already know and states that this approach is ideally suited to the learning needs of young bilingual children. You can see how, in this example, the celebration of culture and language is embedded in the everyday activities. The home corner is equipped with artefacts, printed materials and pictures that reflect this. The books and stories and songs are available in languages additional to English. In an environment like this children are most likely to respond with enthusiasm, interest and respect to the world around them.

Summing up

- Build on the considerable amount of knowledge that all children have learned at home when they come to your setting.
- Show respect for the languages, cultures, religions, home backgrounds and family value systems of the children and their families.
- Provide opportunities for children to share, take turns and become involved in collaborative play.
- Make sure that children are invited to make choices, follow their own interests and get deeply involved in what it is they are doing.
- Help children learn how to ask for help by offering help when appropriate.
- Organise your resources and the routines of the day so that children become independent and are able to get involved in doing 'real' jobs for real purposes.
- Be prepared to show what you think is worthwhile. Give clear signals about what you think is good and what not.
- Help children develop an understanding of right and wrong by always giving clear explanations.
- Allow children to express their feelings, even when these are sometimes difficult for you to handle.
- Offer children a cared-for environment and ensure that they don't come across books with pages missing or puzzles with pieces missing.

- Above all, offer a range of meaningful activities so that children can, through first-hand experience, solve problems, communicate with others, express their feelings and understand the social rules.

LANGUAGE AND LITERACY

You will know that the development of language and literacy is key to children's learning. Children need to be able to express their thoughts and ideas in speech and in writing and they need to gain access to the thoughts and ideas of others through reading. Language pervades every activity that children engage in and since all children are curious, they spend much of their time in the early years trying to understand the symbolic world they encounter. You will remember this from the first chapter of this book. Since language and literacy are essential to children's learning they are areas you need to plan particularly carefully for and areas that nursery inspectors will pay particular attention to.

Two points before we look at the 'Desirable Outcomes'. The first is that children learn language and literacy in the same way that they learn about the physical world and the social world. They pay close attention to what those around them are doing and to what they see and hear around them. From this they try to find some pattern which will enable them to work out the rules that apply. Children do not need to have lessons in how to talk. They talk because they want to communicate and because they hear people talking all around them and discover that speech is the best way of making your needs, desires and intentions clear. The same applies to the written word. Children see print all around them and they begin to wonder what these marks are, why they are there, who made them and why. They begin making marks for themselves and, at the age of about three (although this varies enormously with experience and exposure to print) they begin to describe these marks sometimes as drawing and sometimes as writing. When children are exposed to books and stories they begin to recognise the links between reading and writing: they understand that the marks can be read and that they always say the same thing. So children need to see people around them writing and to have examples of writing to look at. They need to have stories and rhymes read to them and to see competent readers using books. They need time to explore these things for themselves, through play and supported by sensitive interaction. This will foster their learning and understanding far better than instructing children in the letters of the alphabet or the patterns of writing.

The second point is that language does not mean only one language – that is English. Young children will learn most effectively when they are able to build on what they already know. Children who have a language other than English have already acquired this language – in some cases more than one language! They understand how this language works and are able to use it for thinking. Forcing young children to abandon their first language in order to learn English is both insensitive and damaging. Of course young children do need to learn to speak, read and write in English if they are to succeed in the English school system. There is much that monolingual workers can do to support children's home languages and help them acquire English We will discuss this more fully in a later chapter.

The 'Desirable Outcomes' state that, by the age of compulsory schooling, children should:

1. *listen attentively and talk about their experiences both in small and in large groups*

Your setting should be a place where children know that talking to themselves, to one another and to the adults is something that is regarded as worthwhile. There should be opportunities for children to talk about what they are doing, the problems they encounter, the solutions they have come to. Children should be encouraged to talk, but not forced to talk. In schools children sometimes have to endure something called 'news time' where each child is coerced into saying something about what has happened at home over the weekend. This is both socially divisive (what if all that happened to you at the weekend was to listen to your parents arguing or having to help clean up your younger sibling's mess?) and something that young children find difficult to do. Many adults would hate to be put on the spot like that and have to find something to say in front of others. So do encourage talk, but never force it.

It is worth reminding ourselves that the outcomes refer to children once they reach statutory school age. With younger children paying attention to a story in a large group is often difficult and in the best practice children are divided up into smaller groups for story times. This can be done in a number of ways. The worker might invite children to choose which book they want to listen to or choose a group of children who might particularly enjoy, say, a Bengali story.

2. *use a growing vocabulary with increasing fluency to express thoughts and convey meanings to the listener*

The rate at which children's vocabulary grows is stunning. When children start in your setting they are usually able to express their needs and desires, to talk about things that are familiar to them and things that matter to them. They have learned all this in their homes and through listening and interaction. Their learning of new words will continue as they are exposed to new and challenging situations and as they encounter new and unfamiliar words in stories read and told.

There used to be the view that adults should use only simple language with young children in order to ensure that they learn new words easily and don't have to cope with difficult words. You will have noticed, however, that very young children are often fascinated by long words – things like stegosaurus, amazing, helicopter. Adults should use normal speech with young children and this can include long words, complex phrases and technical terms. It is important that when adults use mathematical words – like the names of shapes or words of comparison or position – that they use the correct words. Why tell children that bubbles are 'round' when they are, in fact, spherical? Children can learn the word 'sphere' as easily as they can learn the word 'round'.

Children who have had a rich diet of hearing stories read and told will benefit in many ways. One of these is the learning of new words: another is the learning of the very specific language found in books. This 'book language' is different in form and style from the language of speech. You would never say something like 'the road was long and winding and the light became dimmer and dimmer as we walked'. You might say 'We walked down this long road and it was getting dark'. So the language of books is more complex, more poetic and has its own conventions – things like 'Once upon a time' or 'They all lived happily ever after'. Children need to begin to understand this so that when they begin to make up their own stories they are able to use the language of books in their telling and writing.

3. listen and respond to stories, songs, nursery rhymes and poems

You will know that offering children many opportunities to listen to stories, songs, nursery rhymes and poems is one of the most important parts of your work. There are now hundreds of high-quality children's picture and story books available in a number of formats and children will benefit from hearing familiar and new stories read and told to them individually, in small groups and in larger groups.

Here is how Rainbow Playgroup organise their books and story sessions:

> We have fund-raising events every term with the specific aim of raising money to buy books. We have two book corners in the room and make sure that each is inviting and welcoming. One is large enough to contain a large group of children. It is carpeted and has some bean bags for children to sit on. The other is a much smaller area and is very cosy and secret. Children go in there in ones and twos.
>
> We keep the books on shelves with the front of the book visible to the children. We think this is important in helping them choose which books to read. We also have books in plastic containers and these are on the floor so children can browse through these.

What books do we have? Well, we have all the popular children's picture and story books – several copies of each, in paperback. We also have some large format books – Big Books – that we use with small groups of children to help them come to understand how books work – how you turn the pages, which bit carries the meaning, which direction English print goes. Then we have some information books and some books in English and another language. We don't have enough of those so our aim is to increase the number by the end of this year. We have also made some packs in which we have the book, some story props we have made to go on the magnet board and a tape recording of the story. With the dual text books we have invited parents in to read the story in the other language. This year, for the first time, we have decided to have some 'core books'. The idea is that we choose six books and use these as the basis for a lot of the work we do. We have multiple copies of these and the children – who can take a book home each evening – often choose these. We had a session for parents to explain the 'core book' system and to tell them why we have chosen the books and what the children could learn from the books and how the parents could help, if they wanted to.

The core books include: *The Very Hungry Caterpillar*, *Mr. Gumpy's Outing*, *Not Now, Bernard*, *So Much*, *Ah! Said Stork* and *Where's Spot?*. We chose these because they are books the children really like. Each offers excellent pictures, a text that helps children remember the story and introduces them into the patterns of language. Next term we are adding *Peepo* and *Dear Zoo*.

We often use a story as 'a theme' for a few weeks. This term we are using *The Very Hungry Caterpillar*. We have made a wall story and the children made a caterpillar out of old tights stuffed with newspaper and painted. Then we worked out how to make it move by using a pulley. So the caterpillar can crawl through the food and the leaves. Last term we used *The Three Billy Goats Gruff* and set up a scenario in the garden, using some PE equipment to make a bridge and making models of the troll out of cardboard boxes. The children played the part of the billy goats. Every day we made sure that several versions of the story were set out near the bridge.

The other things we like to do is to set out a 'small world' scenario with the books. So with *Mr. Gumpy's Outing*, for example, we set up on a table a mirror for the lake, a toy boat, toy animals and Lego people, together with the book. We noticed that many of the children – especially the bilingual children – would play with this for ages, retelling the story or making up their own stories.

You will see just how much thought has gone into the provision of books at Rainbow Playgroup.

4. *make up their own stories and take part in role play with confidence*

The staff at Rainbow Nursery used a number of devices to help children make up their own stories or retell familiar stories. A well set-up setting will provide children with numerous opportunities for role play and staff will strive to give children the understanding that role play is something valuable and important and not something you do when you have completed your work.

It is very worthwhile practising your own skills as a storyteller. Telling a story is a different activity from reading one. For one thing you can change the story as you go along. You can use different voices and introduce sound effects. You can include the children in the story. You can get the children to help you find an ending for the story or decide what might happen next. And you can make eye contact with the children and watch their reactions. Children who are fortunate enough to hear a story told and the same story read from a book come to understand that it is the print that makes the story exactly the same on each occasion that a book is read. This is an important thing to learn.

5. *enjoy books and handle them carefully, understanding how they are organised; know that words and pictures carry meaning and that, in English, print is read from left to right and from top to bottom*

Not only do children need to hear stories read and handle books, but they need to come to understand how books work. When very young children first encounter books they have no way of knowing that it is the print that is read. Very young children read the pictures and the writers of books for children take great care that the pictures not only support the story but often tell their own story. Reading the pictures is an important part of learning to read. It is only when adults – often without any direct intention of 'teaching' – draw children's attention to the print that children begin to realise that those black marks have a function. Adults may run their finger under the text as they read or point out a word that recurs or a letter that has some significance for the child – like the initial letter of the child's name. In doing this they make the child aware of the significance of the print.

Children also come to understand that books are written and illustrated by people, and adults can help them by saying things like 'Oh, here's another book by Eric Carle. He's the author of *The Hungry Caterpillar*' or 'I like the pictures in *Peepo*: they are just like the pictures in *The Baby Catalogue*'. Talking about the titles of books, the authors and illustrators, the logos, even the bar codes gives children some understanding of how books are created and what the different parts of the book represent.

It is informative to really pay attention to what young children do when they look at books. Children whose first language is, say, Hebrew, who start looking at a book from the back to the front are not showing their ignorance of how books work. Rather they are demonstrating their understanding of how books work in their first language. Children who sort out all the books with the logo of a lion on it are paying attention to what is the same about certain books. Children who always choose books by one author are demonstrating a preference.

> Hannah, at 14 months, will choose what book to look at. She will scrutinise the pictures, flicking through the pages to find a page that interests her. She will sometimes point at the text and make the sounds of reading. If she wants an adult to read to her she will bring the book and climb onto the adult's knee. She will point to items on the page and make sounds in her attempts to name the items. She will laugh at the funny bits. As she does this she is demonstrating all that she has learned about books and watching her is both informative and exciting.

6. *begin to associate sounds with patterns in rhymes, with syllables, and with words and letters*

This is one of the Outcomes that causes nursery workers some anxiety and it is one where it is important to remind ourselves that the Outcome applies to children once they reach school age. Certainly young children need to be exposed to the sounds of languages and to the patterns they encounter. Nursery rhymes and songs are ideal for this. There is a body of research which shows that children who have a lot of experience of rhyme come to understand the patterns in rhyme and find learning to read easier than children who have not had such experience. So read and say rhymes and songs. Talk about words that sound the same. Make your own Big Book versions of the rhymes children know, writing the rhyme up in front of them. As you do this you are modelling for the children not only how expert writers write English (such things as left to right and top to bottom) but how words that sound the same often (but certainly not always in English) look the same.

Here is an example of how a rhyme can be written up to illustrate some of the above points:

| Humpty | Dumpty | sat | on | a | wall |
| Humpty | Dumpty | had | a | big | fall |

> Adult: Can you see that Humpty and Dumpty look almost the same. What is different about them? Look at 'wall' and 'fall'. Are

they exactly the same? What is different about them? Harry, can you find a word that starts with the same letter as your name?

Clearly this has to be done with sensitivity, ensuring that no child is put on the spot. Invite children to contribute when you know that they can. Harry is very likely to know that his name starts with 'H': after all, he will have seen his name written hundreds of times. So asking him to find the letter 'H' is not putting him on the spot.

Young children are interested in words and in letters and they will enjoy activities related to these so long as the activities are meaningful to them. You will have to decide whether you think that teaching young children the sounds of the letters is an activity that will make human sense to them. Lots of children learn the alphabet by heart and almost all children know the letters that make up their own name and often the names of friends and family. But it is worth remembering that English is not a phonetic language. There are rules, but there are so many exceptions to these rules that young children cannot learn to read by sounding out words. They may be able to sound out words and do what is known as 'bark at print': but reading is about more than decoding the words. It is, essentially, about lifting the writer's meaning from the page. In order to do this, children need to encounter books with adults who will respect the children's attempts to read the book from the pictures, by heart and then by paying attention to words. It is only once children can do this that they can start to pay attention to the individual letters and sounds that make up words.

7. recognise their own names and some familiar words

Most of the children in your setting will recognise their own names and often the names of family members and friends. They may even recognise some words that have particular significance for them. There are many games and songs and stories in which you can put children's names. Children love seeing their names in a story or song and quickly learn to recognise the names of other children.

8. recognise letters of the alphabet by shape and sound

This is another Outcome which may cause you some difficulty. Do remember that this applies to children starting school and you should be wary of trying to teach children the shapes and sounds of letters of the alphabet in any formal and decontextualised way. Having alphabet charts on display (and remembering to include alphabets other than English) is a good idea and it is a good idea to have sets of magnetic letters for children to play with. By all means talk about the letters of the alphabet if children are interested, and support children's attempts to understand them and use them.

9. use pictures, symbols, familiar words and letters in their writing to communicate meaning and show awareness of some of the different purposes of writing

Young children begin to write as part of their exploration of their physical world. Making marks with a finger on a misted window pane or with a stick in the sand, children begin to realise that their hands themselves or a tool used as an extension of their hands can leave a trace. Once children are offered pencils or crayons they discover that the marks they make are permanent. This is a satisfying event and one children are keen to repeat – often with disastrous consequences on walls and floors! Children's earliest marks are not representations of anything, but a record of their physical movements. But as children see people around them engaged in writing they begin to want to discover what it is that these people are doing. So their own mark-making becomes more intentional and the intention is often to communicate some meaning.

When children enter your setting they are often able to say that their marks are either drawings or writing. In other words they recognise the differences between two symbolic systems – a significant achievement in itself! In their earliest attempts at writing they will often include writing-like patterns and letter-like shapes. Do remember that children who have seen adults using Bengali script, for example, will include Bengali letter-like shapes in their writing. This, again, is evidence of children's knowledge and not of their lack of knowledge. As children see more modelling of writing and as they see writing in books, in the setting and in the world around them, their attempts at writing will move closer and closer to recognisable letters. Often the first letters you will recognise will be the letters in the child's name. It is worth paying close attention to what it is the children are doing as they write and it is important to remember that writing is more difficult than reading since it involves the skills of actually forming the letters, words and sentences as well as making up the meaning. In other words, it involves skills that are both secretarial and compositional.

Children are not only working out how the written system works, but also trying to understand the different functions and purposes for writing. They see adults around them engaged in acts of writing for different purposes – a note to the milkman, an entry in a diary, a message on the message board, a letter to gran, a form in the post office and so on. In your setting you should try to offer children opportunities to explore the purposes of writing in as many meaningful ways as possible.

Here, again, is what Rainbow Playgroup decided to do to encourage children to explore the purposes of writing:

Well, first we set up a writing corner. We put up alphabet charts in three languages (English, Bengali and Turkish). We put in an old typewriter, a stapler, a hole punch, scissors, lots of different sizes and types of pencils, crayons, coloured pencils, felt pens. We put out small books of blank pages stapled together, writing paper, strips of paper, envelopes, blank forms. The children often go in there and do their own writing. We notice that they always write in the boxes of the blank forms!

We timetable ourselves so that one of us is always in the writing corner, sometimes writing our letters or shopping lists. The children are always interested in what we are doing and want to have a go themselves.

We try and think of what writing we can put in our imaginative play areas. Last term we had a cafe and the children helped us make signs for the cafe. We wrote up a menu and there were little notebooks for the children to use when they took an order. There were strips of paper for them to use for the bills. One member of staff brought in an old cheque book and the children had a great time writing cheques! One of the children suggested we had a recipe book so the cook would know what to cook and so the children made their own recipe book which included pictures and their attempts at writing or our writing when they wanted us to write for them.

This time we have got a baby clinic and the opportunities for writing include a diary, a weighing chart, writing paper and envelopes, appointment slips and some more blank forms which we got from our local clinic. And it is impossible to separate out reading from writing, so we have lots of leaflets and wall charts and a sign on the desk where the children can slot in their own names if they are 'on duty'. It's been great!

It is really worthwhile thinking about what possibilities for writing (and, of course, for reading and talking) you can provide in your imaginative play areas. When you do that and when you pay close attention to what the children are doing, you are able to allow children to follow their own concerns as they play and help them take the next step in their learning.

10. *write their names with appropriate use of upper and lower case letters*

At the age of five most children will be able to do this, particularly if they have repeatedly seen their names written in this way. When you are writing a child's name it is sometimes worth talking about the fact that names are always written with a capital letter at the beginning. Some children are interested in the fact that the same letter can take two forms and may want to pursue this. Again, however, you should be wary of 'teaching' capital and lower case letters in a decontextualised way.

Summing it up

- Language pervades every area of learning.
- Children learn language and literacy just as they learn about their physical and social worlds, as active learners trying to understand the world they inhabit.
- Children who have already acquired a language other than English should be supported in using this language as they acquire English.
- A good nursery or playgroup is one where children and adults know that talking is respected and valued.
- Adults should use appropriate language which is aimed to help children understand and to move on in their learning.
- Books introduce children to wider worlds and increased vocabulary as well as the very specific language of books.
- All young children should have access to books, rhymes, songs and stories on a regular basis individually and in small groups.
- Children should have opportunities to retell known stories and to make up their own stories. Adults should try telling stories as well as reading them.
- Adults should help children come to understand how books work by drawing their attention to the direction of print, inviting them to turn pages, helping them focus on the print itself and begin to realise that it is people who write and illustrate books.
- Adults can help children find the patterns in language by spending some considerable time reading and creating rhymes, singing songs and encouraging children to play with spoken and written language.
- Adults should, above all, help children realise that, in reading, the task is to lift the writer's meaning from the page. They should help children use all means available to them to understand and then retell the story.
- Adults can introduce children to many aspects of literacy by including children's names in stories, songs, rhymes and games. Children's names are significant to them and using them offers many opportunities for children to learn about letters and sounds.
- Adults should display alphabets and scripts in the languages of the children and should offer children magnetic letters to play with.
- Adults should ensure that they provide many opportunities for children to explore reading and writing through familiar and meaningful situations.
- Adults should model both reading and writing, showing children how expert readers and writers operate.

- Adults should pay close attention to what the children do as they play at reading and writing and use this to inform their planning.
- Adults need to remember that writing is a complex skill involving the aspects of forming the letters and the words and constructing meaningful and grammatical sentences that convey a meaning, as well as the compositional skills of creating the message. So writing involves both the 'how' it is done and the 'what' it says. For young children focusing on both aspects of writing at the same time is extremely difficult. Adults need to be willing to 'scribe' for the children – that is to write down what the children say. Doing this allows children to focus only on the composition and not to have to be concerned with how to write down their ideas.

If you are offering children a print-rich environment with opportunities to talk, read, write in meaningful contexts and with sensitive and appropriate intervention you will be providing a sound foundation for children to reach the Desirable Outcomes by the age of compulsory school age. If, however, you become anxious about the Outcomes and want to 'teach' to them, you run the very real risk of damaging children's desire to continue learning.

REFERENCES

Department for Education and Employment, 'The Next Steps', DfEE, 1996.

Dunn, J., *The Beginnings of Social Understanding*, Basil Blackwell, 1988.

Gregory, E., *Making Sense of a New World: Learning to Read in a Second Language*, PCP, 1996.

Heath, S.B., *Ways with Words: Language, Life and Work in Communities and Classrooms*, Cambridge University Press, 1983.

Katz, L., 'What Should Young Children Be Doing?' in *American Educator*, Summer 1988.

School Curriculum and Assessment Authority, 'Desirable Outcomes for Children's Learning on Entering Compulsory Education', DfEE, 1996.

Smidt, S. (ed.), *'I Seed it and I Feeled it': Young Children Learning*, UNL Press, 1995.

Smith, M., 'Making Honey' in Smidt, S. (ed.) *'I Seed it and I Feeled it': Young Children Learning*, UNL Press, 1995.

Voss, B., 'Supporting Young Children' in Smidt, S. (ed.) *'I Seed it and I Feeled it': Young Children Learning*, UNL Press, 1995.

5

UNDERSTANDING AND EXPLAINING THE PHYSICAL WORLD

Dov (aged four) arrives at the playgroup and hangs his coat on his peg. He then goes over to the book corner and spends about 20 minutes sorting out the books in one of the book boxes. An adult (who has decided to observe Dov for that morning) notices that he is making piles of books of the same size. Satisfied with that he goes over to the junk modelling area and sorts out some things he wants to use. He selects an empty box and a yoghurt carton, together with some brightly coloured wrapping paper. He spends the next hour or so attempting to wrap up his chosen boxes. He manages to wrap the box by placing it in the centre of a large piece of paper and folding the paper so that the entire box is hidden. He fastens the paper down using sellotape. The yoghurt carton causes him more difficulty. He attempts to cover it in the same way as the box, but the shape is difficult for him to manage. The worker notices that he keeps picking up the yoghurt carton and examining it and each time he does this he cuts the wrapping paper. Observing that he will not be successful in this chosen task the worker offers him help, which he accepts. Happy with his wrapped boxes he joins three girls in the construction area and watches what they are doing. He then carefully selects some blocks and proceeds to build a wall. In doing this the worker notices that he starts off using blocks of the same length, but when he runs out of those on the second layer of his wall he resorts to using two smaller blocks which are equivalent to one large block. At tidying up time he joins the girls in carefully stacking the blocks in the correct place. The stencils of the shapes of the blocks placed on the shelves help him to match them. In his story group he happily joins in with the songs and the worker notices that when they are singing counting songs Dov is using his fingers to count on. It is Dov's turn to set the tables for lunch and he is very efficient at setting the table for five children and one adult.

What do you think the worker wrote down about what Dov knows about mathematics?

Dov, like most children of his age, has already learned a great deal about counting, matching, sorting, estimating, shape and space, patterns and solving problems. He has learned much of this at home in the everyday activities which involve mathematics. Here is what Dov's keyworker wrote in her analysis of what he knew:

> Dov can sort and match according to size and shape. He is able to estimate area and used his eye to check on the size of the box and the size of the paper. He understands that two smaller blocks are equal in length to one long block. He knows a lot of number songs and uses his fingers to count on. He understands about one to one correspondence and was able to set the table with one fork, one knife, one spoon, one table mat and one cup for each person. He also knew that the adult setting used larger utensils.

Mathematics is a word that strikes terror in the hearts of many child care and nursery workers. Yet in our everyday lives mathematics is so deeply embedded that we are often unaware that we are using mathematics.

Write down all the things you have done this week which involved mathematics.

Did you come up with any of these things?

- put up shelves
- made sure you were on the correct bus
- worked out how much time you needed to make a journey
- put a casserole in the oven for an hour and twenty minutes
- checked you had been given the correct change
- measured your child
- wrapped a parcel
- followed a knitting pattern
- cut a slice of bread in half

We are all able to do these things without difficulty, just as we are able to pick up a pencil or turn on the TV. Yet all of them involve the skills and knowledge we call mathematics.

In the 'Desirable Outcomes' mathematical knowledge has a high priority – particularly the numerical aspects of mathematics. When your setting is inspected the nursery inspector will want to ensure that children are given plentiful opportunities to sort and match, count and sequence, order and compare and use the specific language of mathematics.

Two points are worth making here before we examine the details of the 'Desirable Outcomes'. The first is that children should be involved in first-hand practical experience of handling, counting, sorting, matching and ordering objects in situations which make human sense to them. The adults working with them should strive to use the correct mathematical language with the children and help children to use this very specific language themselves to describe and explain the processes they are involved in.

The second point is that mathematics is culture-free, in the sense that children, whatever language they speak at home and whatever experiences they have had, will be able to engage in problem-solving activities that are not dependent on using and understanding English. This is only true if the children can see the purpose of any activity or select to use the materials on offer in a way which meets their needs and interests.

The 'Desirable Outcomes' state that at the age of entering compulsory schooling, all children should:

1. use mathematical language to describe shape, position, size and quantity

Sometimes nursery workers think of mathematical language as referring specifically to words like 'circle', 'square', 'big', 'small', 'more', 'less', and 'equals'. They are surprised to learn that comparing things and talking about position are regarded as mathematical.

You might like to read through the next example and underline the words which are mathematical:

Three children are playing on the outdoor climbing frame.

Sunita:	I'm climbing right to the top. I am higher than you.
Soraya:	I can climb even higher. See, I'm the very highest.
Priya:	I am coming next to you then I'll also be the very highest.
Sunita:	Let's go across here. You can follow me. I am going first and then you, Priya and you last [points to Soraya]. Then we can go underneath and hang down.

The children, in their play, were using mathematical language to describe their comparisons of height and also to explore position and direction.

Some workers, on reading this outcome, may try to teach children mathematical terms through decontextualised activities – like asking children to colour all the circles on a worksheet red and all the triangles blue. Compare this type of activity which involves the child in merely following instructions with a self-chosen activity where the child is involved in physically exploring the properties of shapes – as in painting, drawing, selecting materials to make a model.

Piaget talks of two different types of knowledge that children use when they act on objects. He called these 'physical knowledge' (which relates to what children discover about objects they handle) and 'logicomathematical knowledge' (which relates to what children discover when they make comparisons between objects). For Piaget physical knowledge comes from information external to the child – from the direct physical exploration of the objects. The source of logicomathematical knowledge is internal: it is what happens inside the child's head. It is important to note that, for Piaget, the two are intertwined and the child cannot separate out one type of knowledge from another. A child comes to recognise the colour red by comparing objects of different colours and by classifying them. No child is able to classify objects without a great deal of experience of exploring them using both his or her senses and physical exploration of objects. The children on the climbing frame in the example above are physically exploring space and position and have obviously explored these concepts before. Through their physical and sensory explorations they have come to understand the concepts of higher and highest.

In order for children to develop the language of mathematics they need to explore the physical properties of objects in order to classify, sort, match, sequence and count. It is only through doing this in situations that are personally meaningful to them that they are able to internalise the concepts so that they are later able to use this language with understanding. This relates directly to another outcome.

2. compare, sort, match, order, sequence and count using everyday objects

In the best nurseries and playgroups children are offered many opportunities to explore mathematics through meaningful situations. Here are some examples to illustrate this.

In each one you might like to decide what aspects of mathematics the children are invited to explore and how the adults involved have ensured this in their planning and provision:

> The children are baking cookies. Each child has a bowl and a spoon and the adult has written the recipe out in large script and reads it aloud as she helps the children in the process. There are six children in the group and the adult has a cookie tin with twelve sections.

> The class has read the story of 'The Three Bears' and the staff have rearranged the home corner so that is has become the bears' cottage. In the home corner are three chairs of different sizes, three beds of different sizes and three bowls of different sizes.

All the children take turns to help set the tables for lunch each day. They have to set a place for each of six children and an additional place for the adult.

In the garden the staff have set up a bus station and have put a number on each of the cars and trikes.

The home corner has been set up to encourage children to act out domestic routines in sequence. There is a mop and a mop bucket; a broom and dustpan and brush; a washing up bowl and a drying rack and dish cloth.

3. recognise and recreate patterns

All young children are busy trying to understand the world and one of the things they appear to do is to try and find out the patterns that are to be found. We have seen, in an earlier chapter, how very young children acquiring their first language work out that there are patterns which determine the rules that govern spoken language, and that they then apply these rules to all situations. The rule, they guess, for all verbs in the past tense is to add 'ed' to the end of all words. They have discovered this rule from listening to the spoken language around them and hearing that when people talk about the past the general pattern is to do just this.

Mathematics, which is a symbolic way of explaining and describing aspects of the physical world, is highly dependent on pattern and on rules. We classify and sort things according to what features they have in common. A child playing with 6 wooden blocks – 4 red and 2 blue, for example – might sort them according to colour or might line them up in a pattern – 2 red, 1 blue, 2 red, 1 blue – or might even just divide them into two equal piles. As in all early learning, young children need to see patterns in their world and to create and recreate them according to their own interests.

Here are two examples. In each case consider what you think the child is learning about pattern and rules:

The children are at a table threading beads. Each child has been given a card which shows a pattern of beads and has been asked to copy that pattern.

Four children in the block play area have constructed a 'building' and have used cylindrical blocks separated out by small cubes. The adult watching them comments 'I like the pattern you have used – cylinder, cube, cylinder, cube'.

70

4. will be familiar with number songs, rhymes, stories, counting games and activities

Most children coming to your setting will already know some number songs and rhymes. These may be in English or in the languages spoken at home. Young children greatly enjoy singing such songs and chanting rhymes, particularly when they are brought to life either through using props on a magnet board or a felt board, or by using the children themselves. It is worth building up your collection of number rhymes and songs and inviting parents and carers to teach you songs and rhymes you don't yet know and which may be in the languages spoken by the children. And you may want to record these onto tapes so that the children can choose to listen to them when you are not available to sing them. Making Big Books of these songs and rhymes provides an invaluable resource and brings to life the links between literacy and mathematics.

How many of these songs and rhymes do you know?

> One, two, three, four, five
> Once I caught a fish alive . . .
>
> One, two, buckle my shoe . . .
>
> Two, four, six, eight,
> Mary at the garden gate . . .
>
> Five elephants went out to play
> On a spider's web one day . . .
>
> Five currant buns in the baker's shop . . .
>
> Five little speckled frogs sat on a speckled log . . .
>
> There were six little frogs
> Sitting on a well . . .
>
> When Goldilocks went to the house of the bears
> Oh what did her blue eyes see? . . .
>
> Five little monkeys jumping on the bed
> One fell off and banged his head . . .

Stories are another invaluable source for mathematical ideas and concepts. If you take the time to look through some of the books and stories you know well you will find mathematics embedded in the stories. There are many attractive counting books and children may well be interested in these and you should certainly ensure that you have some. But just as reading is about more than simply decoding the words, understanding mathematical concepts comes more through exploring these concepts in situations that children understand than through merely chanting them.

Here are some excellent children's books to consider. Take the time to look at each and see if you can identify what aspects of mathematics are explored through both text and pictures.

> *Where's Spot?*
> *Titch*
> *The Three Billy Goats Gruff*
> *What's the time, Mr. Wolf?*
> *Mr. Gumpy's Outing.*

How did you get on with this task?

Finally, in this section, it is worth thinking about stories you can make up to explore different mathematical concepts. In doing this you should also think of what props you can introduce so that in the telling of your story you give the children physical support for the concepts. Hilary Faust, at the University of North London, has made up many such stories and she insists that, after the telling of the story, the props be left out for the children to play with as they retell the story or create their own story. One of her stories concerns a teddy bear who decides to send his cousin a birthday present. He finds a small bowl (which Hilary shows to the children) and then looks for a box to put the bowl in. Hilary has a collection of boxes, some of which are too small and some of which are too big. There is only one which is 'just right'.

Games are another way of helping children understand number concepts. There are many commercially produced games and you will want to examine them to ensure that they will be relevant and meaningful to the children and that they do not reflect images which are monocultural or even offensive. There are also the traditional games of hopscotch, skipping games, finger plays, circle games and ball/bat/hoop games. In these, the players (including the adults) share the agreed rules and can only change them by negotiating.

You can also make games, and when you do you can ensure that they meet the learning needs you have identified from your observations of the children. Some of the best games derive from the stories you read. Here is an example to illustrate this:

> Jenny, the playgroup leader, noticed that some of the older children
> were interested in large numbers. She decided to make a game based

on the 'core book' the group had been using – *Not Now, Bernard*. The game was essentially a number line and the children had to throw the dice and move the number of steps indicated by the number on the dice. The number line moved from Bernard being ignored by his parents to the monster ending up in Bernard's bed and the number line went from 1 to 100.

The children played the game with enthusiasm, initially always with an adult present, but later on they were able to play on their own. After a few weeks Jenny decided that the children might need some cognitive challenge and so she added some labels to the number line in the form of pictures of the monster roaring. Each time the child landed on one of these pictures they had to go backwards rather than forwards, each time the number of steps indicated on the dice. In this way she was helping the children explore both counting on and counting down.

5. *recognise and use numbers to 10 and are familiar with larger numbers from their everyday lives*

Just as you would ensure that you have alphabets displayed in your room so you would want to have a number line and, if at all possible, a number line for the symbols in other languages. You would also want to ensure that you have magnetic numerals and numbers displayed where relevant and appropriate. Children see numerals around them – on buses, on television, on their front doors and in shops. They are often interested to know what these say and will even include numerals in their mark making.

Some numbers are significant to children and the most obvious ones relate to their ages. **Pat Gura** (1996) gives a lovely example of three-year-old Sean exploring how to represent his exact age of three and a half. In a group of children aged three to six who were talking about their ages and examining a set of numerals, Sean selected the numeral '3' and placed it on the magnet board:

> 'Adult: "Three. That's good. Now what about the half? Shall I show you how to do that?" (Sean nods. Andrew and Joshua move closer.) Next to Sean's three, the adult creates the symbol for "half" with three pieces: "There you are, Sean. Now it says three and a half."
>
> Sean is very pleased but Joshua is enthralled. He promptly copies the three and a half, telling anyone who cares to listen: "That says three and a half". Then, announcing each one as he goes along, he makes four and a half, eight and a half, nought and a half, nine and a half, two and a half. At this point he stops and reads them all back.'

*6. begin to use their developing mathematical understanding to solve
practical problems*

Young children in your setting will already be using their developing
mathematical understanding to solve practical problems. You have only to
observe children playing in the home corner or the outdoor play space or
the construction or creative areas to notice how often they do this. Reread
the example of Dov at the beginning of this chapter to see just how many
practical problems Dov solves in his play.

Greco (1962) gives a fascinating example of just how important it is to
let children actually solve problems for themselves – and that means letting
children think rather than giving them a recipe. The example relates to a
five-year-old boy called Jean-Pierre who lived with his mother, father and
sibling:

> 'Jean-Pierre could count to 30. Each day his mother asked him to put
> out the table napkins for the main meal of the day. On the first day
> Jean-Pierre took out one napkin and put it on one plate. He then
> returned to the cupboard in order to get the second napkin which
> he put on the second plate. In all he made four trips in order to
> match each napkin to each plate. About three months later he
> decided to count the plates and then counted out four napkins.
> This continued for six days.
>
> On the seventh day there was a guest for dinner and Jean-Pierre
> found an additional plate on the table. He took out four napkins
> as usual, but then realised that there was a plate without a napkin.
> Dismayed by this he returned all four napkins to the cupboard and
> started all over again, this time making five trips to and from the
> table.
>
> The next day the guest was no longer there, but Jean-Pierre made
> four trips to the table and he kept up this method for five more days,
> when he returned to his previous method of counting plates and
> counting napkins. Ten days later he was told that there was to be
> a guest for dinner again. This time he counted out his four napkins
> and then returned to the cupboard to get an extra one for the guest.
> And on the following day when it was only the family for dinner he
> calmly counted out four plates and four napkins. The presence of
> guests for dinner never again disturbed his counting system.'

This example shows very clearly how, if children are left to solve problems for
themselves, they show initiative, perseverance and develop confidence in their
own ability to figure things out. You might like to think about what might
have happened to Jean-Pierre's thinking had his mother merely told him each
day to get either four or five napkins for the table.

7. through practical activities understand and record numbers, begin to show awareness of number operations, such as addition and subtraction, and begin to use the language involved

It is worth reading that Outcome again and considering what you regard as the key words in it. For me, they are 'practical activities' and 'begin to show awareness'. There is no suggestion in this Outcome that nursery and playgroup workers should be teaching addition and subtraction to children in an abstract form. You will have children in your setting who are adding and subtracting in their play all the time.

Here are some examples:

Rosie and Shameela in the home corner, setting the table. Rosie counts out the chairs: 'One, two, three, four'. She counts the dolls: 'One, two, three'. Then she says to Shameela: 'Get another chair, Sham. We need five and there's only four here'.

Anneka and Liam are setting the table for lunch. Liam puts out seven place mats and Anneka tells him to take one away because there are only six children at that table.

Paulina and Dean are filling up containers with water. Paulina, talking to herself, says 'Fill it up: needs more water.'

Abi, Darren and Charlotte are handing out slices of orange at circle time. Charlotte turns to the adult and says: 'I need two more pieces for me and Morwen'.

Summing it up

- Children learn about mathematical concepts through their everyday experiences as they try to understand the world in which they live.
- Children entering your setting have already learned a great deal about counting, matching, sorting, classifying, ordering, comparing and sequencing.
- Mathematics is embedded in most of the activities of everyday life. Workers should try to be more alert to the mathematical potential of everyday activities.
- Children who have a language other than English can explore mathematical concepts without being dependent on understanding or speaking English.
- Children should encounter numerous opportunities to explore objects and to be involved in first-hand experience. This will allow them to

move to the stage where they are no longer dependent on handling objects because they can hold concepts in their heads.

- The use of mathematical language is an important part of development. Children should be helped by adults to acquire the specific language of mathematics and adults should listen attentively to children to discover just how much they understand.
- Offering children opportunities to explore mathematical concepts in meaningful situations will help children both build on what they already know and move ahead in their learning.
- Songs, rhymes, games and stories provide an invaluable resource for the development of mathematical concepts and language.
- Opportunities should be provided for children to explore shape, space and pattern.
- Numerals should be displayed and children invited to examine and explore these.
- Adults should pay attention to the marks children make, commenting on number symbols where they occur.
- Just as names are significant to children, so are ages. Workers should explore possibilities for building on children's interest in their ages (and sometimes those of their friends and family members).
- Workers should offer children opportunities to think and to solve problems, rather than giving them recipes or solutions. In this way children are allowed to be inventive, thoughtful and to develop confidence in their own abilities to solve problems they encounter in their play and learning.

PHYSICAL DEVELOPMENT

Most of you working with young children will have considered the opportunities children have to develop their physical control, their mobility and their awareness of space. In the best practice children have ongoing access to some outdoor area where they are able to develop the skills of running, jumping, balancing, climbing, riding small vehicles, pushing, pulling, catching, throwing, sliding and so on. Young children's physical skills develop rapidly and they enjoy their developing prowess which gives them greater and greater control over their environment. Children's fine motor skills also develop rapidly, particularly where children are given free access to a range of tools, objects, construction materials and malleable materials to explore. It is important to remind ourselves of the fact that the more varied experiences children have to explore the physical world the more neural connections are laid down. In other words, the more attention you pay to what you provide for children to use and explore, the greater the opportunity for children to learn.

Let us now look at the 'Desirable Outcomes' for this area of learning. They state that, by the age of compulsory schooling, children should:

1. move confidently and imaginatively with increasing control and coordination and an awareness of space and others and use a range of small and large equipment and balancing and climbing apparatus, with increasing skill

If you read through those Outcomes again, carefully, you will notice that the word 'increasing' occurs twice. For me, that is the key word and what it implies for workers is the consideration of how to plan for progression. In other words, you are not only thinking about how to provide opportunities for the development of physical skills but thinking about how to ensure that children are able to refine and develop these skills through their play.

It follows from this that when you are planning for outdoor play it is important to remember not to offer the same activities and materials day in and day out. If you do this you remove the possibility for children to develop increasing control and awareness. Do remember the theory of 'Match' mentioned in an earlier chapter, which suggests that something new should be added to or removed from a situation in order to take learning forward, but that this change should be carefully matched to the child's interests and needs.

Here are some examples to illustrate this:

A worker at the Rainbow Playgroup noticed that four-year-old Tamina, who was very small for her age, was finding it difficult to join her friends in playing on the climbing frame because she found the height of the first step daunting. The worker placed a wooden block at the base of the steps. She observed what happened and was intrigued to find that, not only did this block achieve her aim of giving Tamina the confidence to climb up the steps, but that the other children used the block as something to leap over when they came down the steps!

The staff at a playgroup working in a church hall with no access to outdoor space set up 'A' frames with planks in order to ensure the children have some opportunity every day to develop some physical skills. Using only two 'A' frames and three planks of wood they are able to vary the layout so that children are offered 'bridges' to walk across, ramps to climb up and slide down and enclosed areas to explore. The addition of objects like blankets, torches, picnic baskets, a steering wheel and some milk crates allow the children to turn the 'A' frames into different environments to explore.

The head of a daycare centre asked her staff to plan what aspects of physical development would be catered for each week. This involved the staff in much discussion about what physical activities the children needed to acquire or refine and what materials and resources they should offer. One planning sheet looked like that shown in Figure 5.1.

What is the role of the adult when children are busily engaged in exploring physical space?

Many workers are so intent on ensuring that children are playing safely (which is, of course essential) that they ignore the possibilities inherent in the situation for intervening appropriately and scaffolding learning.

Read through the case study below and then try and identify where you, the adult, might have intervened in order to extend learning. Try and say what you might have said or done.

Rehan, Jo, Beth and Akinola (who has very little English) are all four years old. They are out in the garden playing on the climbing frame. Rehan is 'in charge'. He is leading the other children and telling them what to do. They follow his suggestions happily until Beth,

---

My theme for the week

Reason: Nicola and Harry were trying to balance things in the construction area. I want to give them the opportunity to explore the idea of balance using their bodies.

What I will need

milk crates
planks
climbing frame
ladder

Outdoor play
week of 28/2

Words I might use

balance
low
high
higher
lower
highest
lowest
slope
angle

My plan

Monday: set up planks and crates. Observe.
Tuesday: do the same, but put a plank as a ramp from the lowest rung of the climbing frame ladder. Observe.
Wednesday: the same, but perhaps raise height, depending on how children respond.

Figure 5.1 Example of a playgroup's weekly planning sheet

climbing up onto the plank which goes from one frame to another, loses her balance and nearly falls. She starts to cry and Jo rushes over to comfort her. Akinola, meanwhile, climbs down, goes inside and fetches a cushion from the book corner which he places underneath the plank. He urges Beth to have another go. She refuses and goes indoors. Jo, meanwhile, starts to hang upside down from the rungs and swings to and fro, shouting 'My head's down! My head's down!' Akinola climbs down and stands beneath Jo watching her in fascination. Then he climbs up again and attempts to hang upside down.

How did you get on?

There are no right or wrong answers because we are all individuals and will see things differently and interact differently. But you will have seen many points at which you might have intervened. For example, Akinola's obvious concern for Beth and his action in fetching the cushion offered the opportunity for the adult to reflect back to him the importance of his action by saying something like 'That was such a thoughtful thing to do, Aki. You were making sure that if Beth fell she wouldn't hurt herself'. Did you also consider the many opportunities in this example for introducing some of the language of position and comparison?

Offering opportunities for the exploration of space on a large scale almost inevitably offers children opportunities for play together. Children need to be aware of other children as they climb and jump, run and ride bikes. They need to take turns on the climbing frame and negotiate who is going to do what. And as they play with other children they use language in a meaningful and active context. Listen to your children as they talk in their play and you will find evidence of this. **Vygotsky** (1978) reminds us that:

> 'Learning awakens a variety of internal developmental processes that are able to operate only when the child is interacting with people in his environment and in cooperation with his peers.'

A final word in this section about risk-taking. The concern for children's safety often overrides everything. Many workers place restrictions on children which limit their opportunities to explore fully. This is not always confined to the outdoor area. Some workers limit the number of children who can play in the home corner or who can use the woodwork bench or who can be at the water tray. Such restrictions remove autonomy from the child and make the child dependent on the adult to define what is possible. You might like to remind yourself that one of the characteristics of play is that it allows children to take risks because children set their own agenda. **Purdon** (1993) writes:

'by taking risks children develop signs of autonomy and hence independent learning . . . independent learners are intrinsically motivated learners. Surely our ultimate aim?'

This is an area which often gives rise to fierce argument between workers. Obviously you need to ensure that the environment you provide is as safe as possible, but you also need to consider whether you have made it so safe that little learning can take place. It is important to allow children to take 'safe risks'. After all, if there are five children in the home corner rather than the four you have stipulated, what is the danger? The danger is that you, the adult, are less in control. The children will regulate themselves. When the home corner becomes too crowded play becomes difficult and the children have to resolve this situation for themselves – an excellent opportunity for problem solving and negotiating. Similarly, when considering outdoor play, think carefully about whether you need to limit the numbers of children on the climbing frame or try to restrict what they do.

2. handle appropriate tools, objects, construction and malleable materials safely and with increasing control

The ability to use tools is essential to life. By tools we mean any of the huge number of objects we use as extensions of our hands in our everyday lives – things like a pen, toothbrush, pencil, broom, lawn mower, computer and so on. Not only are tools an extension of our hands, but also of our minds. If you use a window pole to open a window the pole serves as an extension to your body and enables you to perform something you would not be able to do without using the tool. If you use a pen to write down some ideas the tool acts as an extension of your mind.

In the early years of life – the years described by Piaget as the Sensorimotor Stage – young children spend a great deal of time exploring the objects they encounter. They move on from asking 'What is this thing? And what does it do?' to asking 'What can I do with this? What can I use it for?'. By the time children start in the playgroup or nursery they have often had a great deal of experience of exploring the objects in their world and will continue to do so, refining their skills and enhancing their learning.

It follows from this that skilled nursery workers will pay a great deal of attention to the tools and objects they offer children and to the activities in which these tools and objects are set.

Let us return to Rainbow Playgroup and see how they organise for children's exploration of tools and materials.

The staff set up a graphics area (or writing table) and offered the children the following tools, all in labelled containers or set out on stencils:

- pencils
- a range of felt pens
- crayons
- ball point pens
- rubbers
- Tipp-ex
- scissors (both left- and right-handed)
- a hole punch
- a stapler
- glue sticks
- sellotape
- masking tape
- rulers

In the technology (or workshops area) the following tools are on offer:

- various kinds of glue
- assorted boxes, cartons and containers all sorted according to size and shape
- large sheet of wrapping paper, foil, tissue paper
- scissors
- stapler
- sellotape
- masking tape
- paste spreaders
- elastic bands

In the woodwork area:

- a woodwork bench
- a vice
- a saw
- hammers
- nails and panel pins
- a selection of pieces of wood
- wood glue

A variety of malleable materials (dough, cornflour and water, clay, etc.) offered with all or some of the following:

- a garlic press
- a cheese grater
- wooden rollers
- pastry cutters

- straws
- cookie tins
- knives
- spoons
- forks
- objects that can be used for leaving an imprint (like Sticklebricks)

In the construction area:

- a set of large Community Playthings blocks set out on stencils
- a set of small Community Playthings blocks similarly organised
- a railway set
- several construction toys like Lego, Duplo, Mobilo, etc.
- vehicles
- two wooden planks to act as ramps
- some shiny strips of lino
- some rough strips of cardboard

In their planning notes the staff plan that some of these activities will be set up outdoors each day, offering children the opportunity to develop their fine motor skills both indoors and out.

You will realise just how much thought has gone into planning the resources described above. Some of them are costly (like a woodwork bench and the Community Playthings blocks) but most are not and can easily be gathered together and maintained. It is important that resources are set out in such a way that children can follow their own plans through and find the resources they need without having to call on an adult. Of course adults do need to be on hand in order to interact, to help, to demonstrate sometimes, to observe what the children are doing and to scaffold learning.

The difficult question of safety arises again. Some workers are reluctant to let children use woodwork tools or to use things like a garlic press. Often children are offered scissors which are so blunt that they will not cut. If children are to explore tools and to get involved in the processes they have determined for themselves it is essential that they are offered tools that work and that are cared for. Of course there are dangers, but children are generally sensible and respond well to being given some autonomy. Workers need to show children how to use the tools and explain to them that a saw, for example, is sharp and has to be used with care. They also need to involve the children in caring for the resources so that the next time they want to use them they are still in working order.

You may be interested in two examples of children exploring tools which were observed in a nursery in Emilia Romagna:

A table had been set out for the children with rulers, sellotape, long strips of paper, glue, shiny objects, pieces of cardboard, pairs of scissors and pencils. The children were free to use the materials in any way they chose. Some children spent more than two hours at the table, rolling up strips of paper and gluing them onto other surfaces.

At the clay table a group of children were working with an adult trying to make human figures out of clay. The children were aged between four and six. The adult offered them some simple stands made of two pieces of wood at right angles to each other. This formed a sort of support around which the clay figure could be constructed. When the adult was asked what had prompted her to come up with this brilliant device, she said that she had noticed that the children had difficulty in constructing three dimensional figures out of clay because the legs were often too thin to support the body. As a result the figures made by the children were often two dimensional and the children quickly lost interest in making these, since their intention had been to make three-dimensional figures.

Summing it up

You will all already offer children many opportunities to explore the physical world. The important points to remember are that children need access to as many experiences as possible in order that their learning continues – in other words, in order that they are able to gain increasing control of both their fine and gross motor skills. You will want to consider how you can offer a safe and stimulating environment which allows children to take 'safe' risks.

- Children, from a very early age, explore the physical world through movement and through the exploration of the objects they encounter.
- Physical development has consequences for social development and for intellectual development.
- Workers need to ensure that children are able to develop and refine their existing skills through a carefully planned programme and thoughtful resourcing.
- The role of the adult is more than a supervisory role. As in all areas of learning adults need to observe, to scaffold learning, to interact, to demonstrate, to explain, to listen, to offer help and to support in as many ways as possible.
- Although it is essential to ensure that children play and learn in a safe environment, thought needs to be given to allowing children to take risks in order to become autonomous.
- Workers will want to pay attention to the range of tools and materials they offer to children.

- Collaborative play is easily fostered through physical play, particularly outdoors.
- Workers will want to explain to children how to use tools safely.
- Workers will want to involve children in caring for the equipment in their nursery or playgroup.
- Tools and equipment that are not properly cared for insult the child and limit the child's abilities to fulfil the purposes they have set in their play.

REFERENCES

Abbott, L. and Rodger, R. (eds), *Quality Education in the Early Years*, Open University Press, 1994.

Greco, P., 'Quantité et quotité', cited in Williams, C.K. and Kamii, C. 'How Do Children Learn by Handling Objects', *Young Children*, November 1986.

Gura, P., 'An Entitlement Curriculum for Early Childhood' in Robson, S. and Smedley, S. (eds) *Education in Early Childhood*, David Fulton Publishers, 1996.

Purdon, L., 'An Exploration of the Potential of Structured Play for Early Writing with a Group of Five Year Old Children' cited in Abbott, L. and Rodger, R. (eds) *Quality Education in the Early Years*, Open University Press, 1993.

Robson, S. and Smedley, S. (eds), *Education in Early Childhood*, David Fulton Publishers, 1996.

Vygotsky, L., *Mind in Society: The Development of Higher Psychological Processes*, MIT Press, 1978.

6

EXPLORING THE WORLD AND EXPRESSING IDEAS

The world that children explore from the moment of birth extends wider than the exploration of the people and objects in it. Children also struggle to understand the nature of the world. They want to find out why and how things happen: what takes place in the wider community; how things used to be and how things are in different places. They also use every means available to them to express their own thoughts, ideas, hypotheses and feelings. If we try and break this down into traditional areas of the curriculum we are talking about science and technology, about history and geography and about art, music, dance and drama.

In the 'Desirable Outcomes' the areas of science, technology, history and geography are all grouped together under the heading 'Knowledge and Understanding of the World'. By the age of starting compulsory schooling, children should:

1. talk about where they live, their environment, their families and past and present events in their own lives

In an environment where young children feel encouraged to talk and where the adults engage in proper dialogue with children they will often talk about their own lives and the significant events in their lives. Let us examine two different approaches to this and see which offers children more encouragement to share their thoughts:

It is Monday morning in the reception class. All the children are gathered on the carpet for news time. The teacher starts the ball rolling by telling the children some of the things she did at the weekend. Then she invites the children to join in. Bobby is eager to tell that it was his birthday party and that his parents took him to McDonalds for a treat. Jenny says she went to Bobby's party. Lindiwe and Alice-Jane went to the park. Rian and Vernon and Charlie all watched cartoons on telly. Sukvinder, Georgiou and Alessio remain silent.

It is Monday morning in the playgroup. Lettie, one of the workers, has brought in a photograph of herself as a baby. She has also collected together some baby things for the children to explore. She is hoping that the children will start talking about the baby at home or about when they were babies. She plans to ask parents to bring in photographs of their own children as babies and has invited Dario's mother to bring her new baby in to show the children. She also plans to set up a baby clinic in a corner of the room. The children arrive and all cluster round her picking up the bibs and bottles and baby clothes and are very intrigued by the photograph. 'Look' shouts Sam in glee 'no hair'.

'I didn't have hair when I was a baby' responds Lettie, 'but then it grew and now I have got long hair, haven't I?'

'My baby got hair' contributes Filiz, who very rarely says anything since she is in the early stages of acquiring English.

In the first example, although the teacher has attempted to structure the situation in an interactive way by sharing some of her own experiences with the children, the very formal context of 'telling your news' is perceived by some children as a testing situation. It is also a situation in which there is the very real risk of highlighting the differences between children's lives, making some children feel publicly disadvantaged. In the second example the presence of objects to explore and examine and an implicit rather than explicit offer to share experiences allows the children who are shy or in the early stages of acquiring English to join in if they wish to. The first example could be defined as talking for talking's sake, the second as talking in order to share experiences.

What can you do to help children develop their ideas and knowledge about their own world? Many playgroups and nursery classes build outings into their programme. These can range from outings to the local shops in order to buy the materials for cooking or to the local park or to travel on local transport. Visits such as these allow children to make the links between home and nursery and to build on their prior experience. Older children will enjoy visits to places of interest – perhaps to a building site or to a museum or to see a place of particular local interest. You would obviously link the visit to the children's interests and the ongoing work of the nursery group. In doing this you will think about what you can do, before the visit, to prepare the children to get the most out of it. You will also consider what to do within your setting after the visit in order to allow children to build on the experience. Here are some examples of what workers in different settings have done:

We took the children to the fire station and I took along a camera. When we got back the children all wanted to draw pictures and we agreed that we would make a big book about the visit. We used both photographs and children's drawings and the children, with my help, constructed the text which I wrote up in big print in front of them. This gave them a model of how writing works. I also made sure that I had got together some resources for them to use in their imaginative play – some plastic helmets, two small ladders and lots of lengths of hose pipe.

We took the children to the local market where there is a stall that sells seeds. When we got back we set up a plant stall and the children all planted their seeds and labelled them (using invented writing or copying the letters on the seed packets). We talked about how plants need water and the children were really reliable about looking after their plants. They put prices on them and got out the till and the plastic money. One child got some wrapping paper from the technology area to wrap up the plants she was selling. The next day a parent brought in armfuls of cut flowers which the children could also sell at the stall. It was a great success.

Next to the school there is a lot of building going on. I arranged with the site manager to take a group of children across. The children were fascinated with what was going on. When we got back we set up a section of the garden as a construction site. I got together some pairs of Wellington boots, some shovels and forks and some safety helmets. The children carried over planks of wood and large wooden blocks. Two children set up a 'site office' and asked me for some clipboards. The play went on for weeks and involved a great deal of talk and a lot of writing. It was brilliant!

In addition to planning outings and their follow up, you will want to ensure that you have some books which will extend children's learning about their world. There are many excellent information books available for young children. If you do not already own these in your setting and if funds are limited, you can borrow them from the library. So, if you have set up a baby clinic, you might want to borrow books about babies, if you have set up a garage, you might want books about cars and vehicles. And do remember that things like DIY manuals, placed in your imaginative play areas, will spark off a great deal of talk and exploration.

This Outcome refers particularly to the areas of the traditional curriculum known as history and geography. Please reread the Outcome again and decide what you think the key words in it are. For me they are the four words at the end of the statement: 'in their own lives'. In phrasing the Outcome like this the authors have recognised a principle of early learning that some workers may tend to forget – and that is that young children need to be able to see the significance of what they are doing. In other words, they need to make the links between their lives and their experience and what is offered to them. History, for young children, is very brief – perhaps only as long as their own lives. Some young children will want to know what it was like when mummy was little, but no young children will be able to make any sense at all of a topic offered in the playgroup or nursery which looks at 'Victorian kitchens' or anything like that.

The same is true of the subject of geography. Young children will want to explore their immediate and slightly wider environment and where you have children in your group who have been born in other countries or who have travelled abroad, setting up a travel agent or turning your home corner into a non-traditional non-English home may be very effective. The key is to link what you offer to the children's experience so that they can build on this. This brings us back to the essential tenet of good early years practice – that it builds on individual children's needs, experience and interests and allows children, in situations that make human sense to them, to learn through play and with the sensitive support of adults.

2. show an awareness of the purposes of some of the features of the area in which they live

Visits will help children discover the purposes of some of the features they notice in their environment. Young children, starting in your setting, will already have discovered that shops are there to sell things, that banks are there for people to get money from, that bus stops are where people wait when they want to take a bus. You can build on this knowledge by reproducing some of these features within your setting. Some playgroups have noticed just how play is sustained when they have set up things like a post office, a garage, a bus station, a restaurant or a supermarket within the setting.

3. explore and recognise features of living things, objects and events in the natural and made world and look closely at similarities, differences, patterns and change

In essence, this Outcome is looking at what can be called the 'scientific process'. Anyone who encounters something new, unfamiliar and interesting, struggles to understand it. Young children want to know all sorts of things like why hair grows and grows, how babies are made, why things with wheels roll, why things that are dropped always fall to the ground. In order for them to ask these questions they have to have gone through this scientific process. Let us take the example of the child wondering why things that are dropped always fall to the ground and examine the processes involved.

Basically, what happens is that the child observes something which raises a question in the child's mind. The child notices that an object, when dropped, always falls to the ground. So the child decides to see whether this applies to only some objects or to all objects. The child spends hours (maybe even days) dropping large and small objects. In doing this the child is testing out his or her hypothesis. At some point the child realises that all objects, when dropped, will fall to the ground. In other words the child has arrived at some sort of conclusion.

This process – observing, questioning, hypothesising, testing and concluding – is what scientists do as they try to uncover some of the laws and patterns of the physical and natural worlds. **Susan Isaacs** ran a school in the 1920s which was structured around the principle that young children should be offered a rich and stimulating environment in which they would encounter problems to excite their imaginations and invite them to find solutions. The staff at the Malting House School were all trained to observe children closely and to let children follow their own interests. Susan Isaacs herself wrote a fascinating book (now sadly out of print) in which she records some of the observations and gives dramatic evidence of children learning and developing through their own explorations and the responses of the adults. One of her most fascinating examples concerns the death of one of the rabbits at the school. When the children came in one morning and found the rabbit lying in its hutch they discussed whether or not it was dead. Then one of the children said he knew how to find out. He said they needed to put the rabbit in water to see if it floated. His hypothesis was that dead things sink and living things float. The children put the rabbit in the water and noticed that it moved in the water. They concluded that the rabbit was still alive. Now Susan Isaacs, working with these children, helped them make the next step in learning and understanding. She brought the children a twig, which all the children agreed was not alive. The children put the twig in the water and it, too, was moved by the currents in the water. The children were able to realise that it was the current which had moved the rabbit and that the rabbit was, indeed, dead. What happened next arouses strong feelings in some readers. The children buried the rabbit, but a few days later started to hypothesise about whether the rabbit was still underground or if it had gone 'to heaven'. Susan Isaacs allowed the children to dig up the dead rabbit, which they examined with great interest and a huge amount of passionate discussion.

The children in your setting will be behaving like little scientists in many situations. To stimulate their curiosity and learning you might like to consider what situations and resources will best enhance this learning. Here are some examples to illustrate ideas:

At the Rainbow Playgroup they have paid attention to the resources they can gather together to offer opportunities for children to behave scientifically. The resources include things like batteries, bulbs, magnets, mirrors, motors and gears, pumps and torches, screwdrivers, sieves and tubes. They have gathered together collections of things – things that roll, things that reflect, things that stretch, things that are transparent. They ensure there is a good range of natural objects, living things, found objects and to help children refine their skills of observation they supply midispectors and magnifying glasses. To help children explore sound they offer things to bang, to pluck, to vibrate, to scratch and to shake.

Staff have noticed that children's play in the sand has become rather repetitive. They set out the sand in two small containers – one with wet sand and one with dry. On the table next to the trays are some miniature scoops, some tea strainers, some shiny objects, some cut up straws and some small moulds.

The Mobilo joining pieces have stretched and the children are having difficulty making models. The staff remove these pieces and put out, instead, some paper clips, some elastic bands and some masking tape.

In the last two examples you will notice that the staff do not have any specific teaching point in mind. Rather they are interested to see how the children use the materials offered to solve the problems implied by the materials but determined by the children's own interests.

4. talk about their observations, sometimes recording them and ask questions to gain information about why things happen and how things work

Where you, the adult, are present as children act like little scientists and indicate that you are interested in their ideas, you will encourage them to talk about not only what they notice but also about their hypotheses. You will remember the example of the child trying to make honey in an earlier chapter and have noticed how the adult was able to encourage him not only to go on discovering, but also to share his thoughts.

Encouraging children to ask questions is not difficult. There are some children who ask so many questions that you feel you want them to stop rather than encourage them to keep going! It is important to realise that some of the questions children raise are not always put in the form of questions. You have to be very alert to the child's purposes in order to spot the hidden question. To illustrate this, here is an example:

Donna is constructing in the brick area. She is trying to make a bridge. She gathers together some cylindrical blocks and places

90

them in a line with spaces between them. She then gets a plank of wood to lay across the top of them. The plank she has chosen is too short to cover all the cylinders. She stops, looks carefully, tries the plank two or three more times and then carefully removes two cylinders. This time the plank fits.

Can you see how, in this example, Donna is questioning her own construction and arriving at a solution?

If you want to encourage children to communicate their thoughts and findings you will also want to consider what support for this you can provide. In the Froebel Block Play Project, a group of researchers were examining how children approached and solved problems through playing with blocks. They noticed that providing children with the means to record their findings and sometimes modelling this for the children stimulated a great deal of recording. Many people working with young children now offer clipboards as a regular piece of equipment in the block play area, the outdoor areas, the home corner and so on.

> 5. *explore and select materials and equipment and use skills such as cutting, joining, folding and building for a variety of purposes*

Children are only able to select the materials and tools for a task if they are given the opportunity to do so. You will remember the emphasis earlier in this book on offering children a properly set-out environment in which children can independently find the materials and tools they need. (To remind yourself of this you might want to read again the relevant section in the previous chapter on Physical Development.)

This outcome refers particularly to the area of learning in the traditional curriculum called technology. Here, just as in science, the process the child goes through in making an object or constructing an environment is what matters. The process involves planning what to make, choosing the materials and tools for the task, making the environment or object, reviewing it and making changes where necessary. If you reread the example of Donna above you will see that she planned to make a bridge; she selected the blocks she would require; she started making her bridge; she reviewed the process and made changes. If a clipboard had been provided she might have taken the process a step further and recorded her construction.

Here is how Rainbow Playgroup have planned for 'technology' in their organisation and resourcing:

> We set up a 'workshop area' and involved the parents in bringing us materials for this on a regular basis. At first all the empty cartons and boxes were just dumped into a large container, but we discovered

that the children were just taking the thing at the top and not making proper choices. So we rearranged this and managed to get the parents to put their offerings in the correct container. We have several large plastic containers and they are labelled. All the toilet rolls and long cylinders go in one: circles (lids and things like that) in another; large boxes, small boxes, tubs and so on. Then we have made stencils and put things on them: a stapler, sellotape, masking tape, pairs of scissors, rulers and so on. We mix glue every morning and children know that they can go and get the woodwork glue from the work bench if they need it.

As well as all this we collect attractive things and store these in labelled containers – things like sequins, beads, bits of fabric, cut up wrapping paper, pictures, small objects the children bring in, feathers, ribbon and so on. Then we also provide lots and lots of different sizes and shapes of paper. We have rolls of foil, sheets of wrapping paper, sheets of shiny paper and sheets of tissue paper. We explain to the children that these are expensive and should be used with care. We were amazed at how responsive the children were. Sometimes we hear them saying things like 'I'm going to use some of that 'spensive shiny stuff 'cos this is for my mummy!'

The technology area was the first area of our room we paid attention to and it remains very popular with the children. We often timetable an adult to be there, but even when no adult is actually based there we set it up in the mornings with something slightly different each day. The children spend a very long time in there, getting deeply involved in what they are making. We have noticed that it is an area where there is a lot of talk going on and are aware of the fact that, since it is not dependent on children being able to speak English, all the children in the room use it.

6. use technology, where appropriate, to support their learning

Not all settings have access to computers and many that do offer the computer as 'an activity', not necessarily thinking about how to use it as a tool for children to use to support their learning. There are now many programmes produced particularly for young children, but if you use these you need to examine them and consider just how they support learning.

Young children will enjoy just playing with the keyboard and watching what happens on the screen when they press keys. This physical exploration is an essential stage of learning and children who do this are not 'messing about'. Adults can certainly interact with children as they explore the effects of their actions, explaining the purpose of keys and symbols. Older children may attempt to find particular significant letters on the keyboard – perhaps those to be found in their names. You will recognise that the symbols on the keyboard are upper case letters; you may want to buy or make a template of lower case letters to fit over the keys.

Young children will also enjoy the effects of using one of the many paint programmes available, particularly if you have access to a colour screen and colour printer.

A final word: do try and monitor which children use which areas of your room. In some playgroups boys still dominate the computer, the woodwork area and the construction area, with girls dominating the writing area, the book corner and the home corner.

Summing it up

Knowledge and Understanding of the World encompasses a very wide area of learning and development. Providing for this learning is a vital part of the role of any playgroup or nursery worker. One of the best ways of doing this is to remember that children learn best where they are able to see the point of what they are doing and where they are able to build on what they already know. A topic about babies will be more meaningful to young children than one about 'Schools in 1900', for example.

- As young children strive to understand their world they want to know about how and why things happen; about people and their relationships; about their own lives and families both now and in the 'touchable' past.
- Workers will want to help children find answers to the questions they raise by setting up meaningful contexts within the setting; using appropriate information books and taking children on visits and outings into the local community.
- Workers will show an interest in children's developing ideas and concepts and will encourage children to talk about these in context rather than in testing situations. They will also provide materials for the children to use to record their ideas should they wish to do so.
- Workers will want to ensure that they provide many opportunities and resources for children to behave like little scientists.
- They will also offer an environment which supports children making choices in terms of materials and resources.
- Workers may set up an activity or area with some specific aim in mind, but need to accept that children may follow their own agendas and that this is perfectly acceptable.
- Where a computer is available it should be regarded as a tool to extend learning rather than as a separate 'activity'.
- Workers need to remain alert to ensuring equality of access and opportunity within all the activities on offer.

CREATIVE DEVELOPMENT

You will remember that **Loris Malaguzzi** talked of 'the hundred languages of children', by which he meant the many ways in which children can express their ideas and thoughts and findings (see p. 35). Young children need to be able to explore the world and express their findings in as many different ways as possible. This representation and re-representation of their ideas is an essential ingredient in learning.

In our society – and particularly in our schooling – we tend to place a far greater emphasis on the skills of reading, writing and numeracy than we do on the creative areas of music, dance and art, for example. Yet if you consider what enriches your life, you will probably include things like listening to music, looking at pictures, going to the cinema or theatre, dancing. The music you enjoy and the films that please you may be different from those that please your best friend – but one of the things that makes us human is that we are moved by the ways in which other people are able to express their thoughts and ideas and feelings using whatever means they choose.

Young children who are fortunate enough to grow up in a society which values such creative expression are exposed from an early age to things of beauty. The children, cited in an earlier chapter, visiting the cathedral in Modena, were able not only to look at beautiful things but to have a go for themselves at expressing their ideas through drawing, painting, mime, dance, imaginative play, music and three-dimensional work. Each attempt at re-describing or re-representing ideas refined children's concepts. It is important to remind ourselves at this point of the importance of what Malaguzzi describes as 'the journey' that children take as they attempt to represent their ideas and feelings. This, the process, is what determines the quality of the learning. The better the journey, the deeper the learning. This applies to children making marks on paper, constructing three-dimensional objects or structures, moving in response to music or any other situation in which children become deeply engaged in expressing their ideas, thoughts and feelings.

Let us now look in detail at the 'Desirable Outcomes' which state that by the age of starting compulsory schooling children should:

> *1. explore sound and colour, texture, shape, form and space in two and three dimensions. They respond in a variety of ways to what they see, hear, smell, touch and feel*

In considering the opportunities you already provide for children to explore their world and the objects in it, you will become aware that this particular Outcome refers not only to creativity, but also to exploration and science, mathematics and physical development. Young children, being inherently curious, explore everything they encounter. In doing so they inevitably pay attention to how things are similar, how things are different. A child pre-sented with three balls, two of which are blue and one green, will perhaps pay attention to colour. The child offered three balls, one rubber, one wool and one plastic may pay attention to texture. This Outcome offers a good example of just how difficult it is to describe young children's learning in terms of subject areas or areas of learning.

It follows from this that children need to be in an environment in which there are interesting things to explore. In the Italian nursery schools described earlier staff collect 'beautiful' things for the children to touch, to examine and to explore. Together with these they offer a range of magnifying glasses and materials for painting, drawing, and three-dimensional work. You may want to think about how you can give children the experience of seeing paintings or sculpture or artefacts. One way to do this is to take children on outings to interesting places. Some nurseries take small groups of children to art galleries and museums. Another way is to get together a collection of posters, books or postcards. A third way is to invite parents to bring in objects that they find interesting or beautiful and to share these with the children. In one nursery school a teacher collected various artefacts from her holiday and brought these in for the children to touch and look at. They were simple things like shells, a length of batik fabric, a small doll, a local musical instrument.

Do the children in your setting listen and respond to music? Young children hear music all around them and many children respond to music by singing, moving to the music, using parts of their body to emphasise the rhythms. Do try and ensure that your children are invited to listen to many different types of music. It is easy nowadays to get hold of tapes of music from all over the world and you might want to think about putting a tape recorder with a selection of taped music in the home corner. Some workers still have a 'ring time' and in one setting this was often used as the time to introduce a tiny snatch of classical music to the children. Whilst the children were passing round their morning fruit, the teacher put on a brief excerpt of music and talked to the children about it. Even the youngest children were responsive.

2. use a widening range of materials, suitable instruments and other resources to express ideas and to communicate their feelings. Through art, music, dance, stories and imaginative play, they show an increasing ability to use their imagination, to listen and to observe

We want children not only to respond to the creations of others, but to have as many opportunities as possible to be creative themselves – that is to express their own thoughts and feelings in any way they choose. We are back to the 'hundred languages of children'.

You will want to ensure that, in your setting, children are able to express their personal feelings through art (painting, drawing, collage, using clay, making things), through music (singing, playing musical instruments and making up their own musical patterns), through movement (responding to sounds and music, using gesture and mime and dancing) and through story (responding to stories, creating their own stories and acting out stories in their imaginative play).

Let us take each of these areas in turn and suggest what materials and activities might promote children's learning.

Art

John Matthews (1994) examines young children's drawing and painting and shows, in his book, how these expressive acts can play a central role in the development of cognition or understanding and in the development of feelings:

> 'When children draw and paint they move through an important sequence in thinking and feeling. We have seen that there is an important mathematical aspect and that language is involved. Drawing and painting extend language, if adults talk intelligently with children about their drawings and paintings. Language organises drawing, and it might be that all representation owes much to the syntax of language.'

Matthews looked at his own children's development and paid close attention to exactly what it was the children were attempting to describe or express. He noticed that the children's involvement in their painting and drawing was deepened where the adult concerned was able really to tune into whatever it was the child was paying attention to. Matthews reminds us that not all paintings or drawings are representational. They may not aim to represent something, but may simply reflect the child's absorption in the effects of his or her own movement, or the effect of mixing colours or what happens when two shapes are placed close together. This is an important point and one that many adults find difficult to grasp. We are so used to considering paintings as being 'of something' that we focus almost entirely on the end product.

Let us look at an example to see how the involvement of the adult can affect the involvement of the child:

> Four-year-old Martin was drawing in the playgroup. The adult came over and asked him what he had drawn. He ignored her, folded up his piece of paper and went outside to play.

The next day an adult was seated in the painting area of the playgroup observing two children. Martin came over and asked what she was doing. She explained that she was watching what the children were doing because she was interested in them. Martin put on an apron and proceeded to paint a thick red line around the edges of the paper. He then chose yellow and made some yellow dabs in the centre of his 'frame'.

'I like those dabs you are doing, Martin' commented the adult.

'Yeah' said Martin, picking up the brush in the green paint 'and now I'm doing green dabs – dab, dab, dab.'

He stood back to observe his painting. Then he carefully selected the red brush again and started to paint a series of vertical lines. 'These are lines' he announced.

'You have done a red frame and now you are doing red lines' commented the adult.

'And then I am going to do some red dabs.'

You will have noticed how the adult, by commenting on what Martin was doing, was able to maintain his interest and let him make choices and decisions. In this way the language the adult used scaffolded Martin's learning and allowed him to be able to reflect on what he was doing. His interest in the activity was sustained through the adult attention. By contrast, where the adult questioned Martin about what his pictures was of, he lost interest and left the drawing area.

You will want to ensure that you offer children high-quality materials that are properly cared for and you will want to involve children in caring for these materials. Here is a list of what you might want to provide:

- surfaces to paint on (sometimes easels, sometimes on the floor or table: paint behaves differently on an easel from on a horizontal surface);
- a range of types of paper (paint, crayons and pens produce different effects on absorbent paper, shiny paper, cartridge paper, etc.);
- felt pens of different thicknesses; pencils; drawing pencils; water colour; poster paint; finger paint; acrylic paint; charcoal (each requires a different technique and produces a different effect);
- thick and thin paint brushes; paint rollers;
- clay and tools for using with clay;
- materials for making things.

Music

You will want to encourage various things in providing opportunities for children to explore music. Firstly you will want to help children, through listening to music, to respond in a personal and creative way. So you will want to offer children opportunities to listen to a range of music and respond to their reaction to the music in a way which focuses on what the child is paying attention to. You may comment on the fact that the child is clapping in time to the music, or that the child has noticed that the music is fast or that the child feels that the music makes him or her feel sad.

You will want to offer children opportunities to make music for themselves. You will ensure that singing songs is an integral part of your curriculum and that you include in your songs those reflecting the languages and cultures of the children. You will want children also to have access to a range of things to pluck, bang, scrape, blow, shake and vibrate. There are many very attractive musical instruments available nowadays and many of these will be familiar to children from their own homes and communities. It is important that children have ongoing access to these instruments. It is only through their own explorations of the instruments that they will discover what the instruments do and what the effects of their own body movements will have on the instruments. You may want to offer children opportunities to make their own musical instruments and to have a go at 'writing' music just as they 'write' stories. In order to do this you would make sure that children can find examples of written music (song books provide an excellent example) and that they have manuscript paper on which to write.

Here are some examples of how some playgroups make music an integral part of their curriculum:

> We went on a course where we learned some musical games to play with the children. So at story time we often incorporate these games in our session. One of them involves singing a song around the group about the children's names. We sing 'My name is Annie. What is your name?' and the child sings back 'My name is Nikiwe. What is your name?' and points to another child. Then we sometimes give the children instruments and ask them to follow the 'conductor' who uses her hands to signal loud and soft – raising the hand means loud, lowering means soft. On one occasion we asked the children to find anything in the room that would make a sound (and we had removed the instruments). They were amazing. They brought spoons to bang together, elastic bands to vibrate, blocks to knock together, corrugated card to strike, paper to crinkle. And sometimes we tell them to watch the conductor and to join in when the conductor points to them. Then sometimes we start off with a rhythm, just using body parts, and ask them to join in.

> We now have a music corner and have in there our tape recorder and a selection of tapes. We have a range of musical instruments (bought out of the proceeds of our last jumble sale). We have made a

'music collage'. This is a large piece of card on which we have stuck things that will make a sound. We have a piece of corrugated card with a lollipop stick hanging next to it on a piece of string; milk bottle tops which jangle against each other; and a range of other things to bang, pluck, scrape and rattle.

We used the song 'Ten Green Bottles' as the starting point for a series of activities. The children all know the song and we often act it out. Then we made a Big Book of it and the children drew the pictures. Then we got ten green bottles and filled them with different amounts of water and set them out (making sure they were in a safe place) together with some beaters. The children were fascinated by how they could 'make tunes' by playing the bottles.

Dance

The exploration of space, using their bodies, is an essential part of early learning for most children. Where children have music to listen and respond to and are encouraged to move – in any way they choose – to the sounds they hear, they use movement as a way of expressing their own ideas and feelings. Some workers believe that any movement or dance session needs to be highly structured. You will have to make your own decision about this. These contrasting examples might help you in this:

All the children have taken off their shoes and socks for a 'dance' session. The adult gets them all sitting quietly on the floor and tells them she is going to play them some music and she wants them to listen to the music and move 'quietly'. She also reminds them that when she claps her hands they must all stop and sit down. She takes the children through a series of movements – moving slowly and quickly, moving high up and low down, tiptoeing and stamping. She often models the movements for the children.

The worker invites any children who want to come and dance to join her in the small room. The children take off their socks and shoes. Music is already playing when they come in and the children join in enthusiastically, each moving in their own way to the movement. The adult moves amongst the children, commenting on what they do. 'Marko, what a huge leap you made' and 'I love the way you are twisting your arms to the music'. When the short excerpt comes to an end she invites the children to suggest what sort of music they want next. One suggests 'loud'; another shouts out 'Bob Marley' and a third says 'songs'. A decision is reached and the children, again, move to the music. Finally, the worker tells the children she has brought in some new music – something she really likes and that reminds her of when she was a little girl and used to go to the seaside with her grandparents. She plays the tape and the children listen, some clapping, some joining in the song.

Stories and imaginative play

You may have come across the work of **Vivien Paley** who uses storytelling as the main means of learning in her classroom. She encourages the children to make up their own stories in order to make sense of their lives and her books (which are fascinating and easy to read) show just how powerful storytelling is in terms of learning and reflection. Paley, through a long personal struggle, discovered that offering children opportunities to construct and act out stories allowed them to confront many issues in their lives and sort out their responses to these. She also discovered that children, in acting out through play, offered her a window into their development.

You will already offer children many opportunities to make up stories as they play in the home corner or other areas in your room. Try and ensure that the props you offer help to take children's storying and their learning forward. Younger children, more concerned with reenacting domestic roles, will need access to 'real' things to help their play, but older children can use lengths of fabric, strips of hose pipe, empty containers – anything, in fact – to become whatever they desire.

A LAST WORD

If you read through the Outcomes in this section you may agree that the key word is the word 'increasing'. Children will already be expressing ideas and feelings in every way they can. The important thing for workers is to take careful note of what children are doing so that activities can be provided to help children refine their skills and increase their range of experiences. Each representation and re-representation brings about this development. The more the opportunities for expressing feelings and thoughts, and the more sensitive the intervention of the adult, the more chance there is that children will develop the abilities to use their imagination, to listen and to observe.

Summing it up

The things that enrich our lives are often things which arise out of our own creative efforts or of those of other people, yet in our schools the expressive aspects of learning have a low status. In our settings for young children we can remedy this by ensuring that creative development is as important to us as cognitive development.

- Young children need as many opportunities as they can get to try and describe and represent their ideas and feelings.
- When children are engaged in representing and re-representing their thoughts and feelings they are involved in solving problems, in selecting appropriate tools and materials, in cognitive development.
- The journey the child takes in representing thoughts and feelings is more important than the final destination. In other words, it is the process that is important to the child.
- Children need to experience and explore painting and drawing, music, movement and dance, gesture and mime, storytelling and imaginative play. These should be regarded as some of the 'hundred languages' of children.
- The role of the adult is, as ever, complex. It involves setting up the environment and resources; modelling; using language to scaffold learning; offering help and advice where needed; tuning in to what it is the child is paying attention to; intervening sensitively.

REFERENCES

Gura, P. (ed.), *Exploring Learning: Young Children and Block Play*, PCP, 1992.
Isaacs, S., *Intellectual Growth in Children*, Routledge and Kegan Paul, 1930.
Matthews, J., *Helping Children to Draw and Paint in Early Childhood*, Hodder and Stoughton, 1994.
Paley, V.G., 'On Listening to What Children Say', *Harvard Educational Review*, 56(2).

7

ENSURING EQUALITY OF ACCESS AND OPPORTUNITY

Ensuring that all children – whatever their background, their experience, their gender, their culture, their religion, their ability – are offered equality of access and opportunity to the curriculum and to your time is a fundamental principle of high-quality early learning. Starting with a knowledge of the children in your group and keeping in mind each individual as you plan ensures that you do this.

Ensuring equality of access and opportunity is so important that a consideration of how to do this flows through each chapter of this book. We consider what resources to provide to reflect the languages and cultures of the children in your group. We talk about planning related to the observed knowledge and interests of the children. We discuss the importance of allowing children to build on what they already know. We examine the dangers of stereotyping children and their families. And in later chapters we look at how to set up partnerships with parents and consider ways of making your setting 'user-friendly' to all users and potential users.

The purpose of this chapter then is not to think about how to provide equality of access and opportunity, but rather to consider the philosophical and human reasons for doing so.

If you read through the 'Desirable Outcomes' you will find little or no mention of the importance of ensuring that all children have equal access to all the activities and to your time. The accompanying booklet 'The Next Steps' does, however, refer to this. In the section devoted to Self-Assessment (that is the process of self-evaluation all settings are required to carry out before an initial inspection) two mentions are made as follows.

Under the heading 'Special Educational Needs Policy and Provision', settings will need to answer the following questions:

a: What is the setting's policy for special educational needs? How is the policy related to the 1994 Code of Practice on the identification and assessment of special educational needs.
b: Is the policy known, agreed and implemented by all staff?
c. What support is available for children with special needs?

Under the heading 'Equal Opportunities':

a: Settings will need to consider whether their educational programme and their working practices promote equality of
access and opportunity for all children to learn and make progress whatever their age, gender, attainment, ethnicity, special
educational need or competence in English.

b: Settings will need to consider their policy for equal opportunities, the arrangements for its oversight and the effectiveness
of its implementation.

c: Settings will need to answer the following questions:
   1: what are the arrangements for equal opportunities?
   2: are those arrangements known, agreed and implemented
   by all staff?

When you consider the realities of your day-to-day work in your own setting
and look around at the range of children you work with, you might want to
question whether this area is given enough prominence in current policy. In
every setting throughout the country there are children who, for one reason or
another, are 'systematically disadvantaged because of their classification as
female, black or working-class or a combination of these categories'
(**David**, 1990). Those working with young children have a position which
is both privileged and carries a huge responsibility. Any setting can be
described as a microcosm of the wider society and within the little community of the setting, the adults have the possibility to shape and build a set of
values and attitudes that may challenge those of the wider society.

POLITICALLY CORRECT OR EDUCATIONALLY ESSENTIAL?

*Have a quick look around your room and ask yourself what it feels like to be a girl, a
black child, a child from a working-class family, a child who is a refugee, a child
whose home language is not English. Can you, as this child, find things that are
familiar? Do you see images of children like you?*

Why bother to consider issues of equality and access? You might want to jot
down why you think it is important. There are many reasons. Some of these
are personal or professional in nature (as where, for example, you believe that
you have a professional duty to cater for all the children you care for) or even
moral and human in intention (as where, for example, you believe that as a
human being it is incumbent upon you to make sure that all children are
treated equally). Many are actually grounded in legal requirements. In
other words, considering the opportunities for all children is not something

you can just choose to do in order to be 'right on' or politically correct. You have a legal obligation to do so under several acts of law.

The Children Act (1989) states that 'Children have a right to an environment which facilitates their development' and then goes on to address children's rights in terms of their sense of identity, which includes the right to individuality, respect, dignity and freedom from discrimination. If, in answering the questions that started this section, you felt that some children in your group might not feel that their particular sense of identity was overtly respected, you need to question whether you are, indeed, offering genuine equality of access and opportunity.

Further, the Rumbold Report (DES, 1990) insists that:

> each institution should have:
> (a) a policy outlining aims and objectives based on a clearly articulated philosophy shared by educators and parents.
> This should incorporate:
> (b) a policy on equal opportunities for children and adults, encompassing sex, race, class and disability, which promotes an understanding of cultural and physical diversity and challenges stereotypes and which is responsive to local needs . . .

You can see from all of this that you need to have a policy on equal opportunities which you, as a group of workers, have agreed on and which you have shared with both children and parents. (We will return to this in the final chapter of this book.) This policy needs to look at a number of issues, as follows:

- Your own attitudes and beliefs and prejudices. This is the essential starting point. You cannot devise and implement a policy on equal opportunities until you have examined and sometimes challenged your own views and ideas.
- A clear understanding of the children in your care – their home backgrounds, previous experiences, religious and cultural values, languages spoken, and other aspects of experience.
- A survey of the resources you provide in order to examine them for stereotypical images and for monocultural or monolingual bias. In other words, do the books, jigsaws and pictures show positive images of girls, of black children, of children with disabilities, of boys, of working-class children? Can children find examples of their home languages in the books or tapes or wall displays in your room? Are images of Africa, for example, true to life, or do they depict Africa as a place where wild animals roam and people live in mud huts?
- A survey of the activities you offer in order to assess whether they invite all children to partake or in some way suggest that certain activities are

only open to certain children. Obvious examples are areas like the home corner (do boys play there?) and the block play area (do girls play there?).

- An exploration of how you handle incidents like name calling, bullying and teasing? Have you all agreed on a policy and do you all implement it equally?
- A consideration of attitudes within your setting. Ask yourself these questions: Do children feel valued? Do their parents feel valued? Are children beginning to be tolerant of the feelings of others? Do you foster co-operation rather than competition?
- A consideration of how parents are involved in the work of your setting.

Reading through this list you might realise that providing a curriculum based on meeting the observed needs of all the children in your group – a developmentally appropriate curriculum – will ensure that you offer equality of access and opportunity. Where you are aware of each child as an individual with a unique and important history and where you seek to build on this in the activities and resources you offer, you will be providing the broad and balanced curriculum recommended in the Rumbold Report. You do, however, need to know something about how social class, gender and race can provide the basis for discrimination if you are to have an effective and meaningful equal opportunities policy.

SOCIAL CLASS

It is a truism to say that those working with young children need to know the children well. What is sometimes ignored, however, is how this knowledge about children is acquired. Sometimes workers make judgements about children on spurious grounds. They judge that a child will not be successful in school, for example, if the child comes from a local council estate or if the child comes from a single-parent family or if the child's parents are unemployed. Attitudes like this reflect a deficit and stereotypical view of working-class families and often result in the self-fulfilling prophecy. The workers or teachers assume these children will fail, and because they are unable to engage with the children's home experience, ensure that the children do fail. There are many studies you can read to illustrate this (**Walkerdine** *et al.* (1989), **MacGilchrist** (1992), **Anning** (1991).)

One of the most obvious areas in which social class emerges as a factor is in terms of language. Some years ago it was believed that children coming from so-called working-class homes encountered an inferior form of language within their homes. **Basil Bernstein**, a sociologist, said that middle-class families used what he called an 'elaborated code' of language, whilst working-class families used a 'restricted code' of language. What he meant by this was that speakers using the restricted code were more dependent on the immediate context in which the language took place. Working-class children, he argued, always refer to things in the here and now, things that can be seen and touched and heard. Children exposed to the elaborated code, he said, were able to move away from this and were not dependent on a shared context in order to communicate. Now since the language used in schools and in education is often about things that are not to do with the here and now and are not dependent on the current context, working-class children are at a disadvantage. This type of view – that of citing the blame for failure within the educational system with the child and the child's family – is a deficit view and one that has been severely challenged since Bernstein's work. You have come across the work of **Tizard and Hughes** and of **Gordon Wells** and will know that they found that all homes provide language which enables children to talk, to think, to solve problems and to communicate.

Despite all this, deficit views of working-class families still prevail and it is still a fact that working-class children do less well within the educational system than those from more privileged homes.

GENDER

The process of learning about gender begins very early. **Weis and Worobey** (1991) believe that children, before the age of three, have already developed what they call 'scripts for their gender'. When you watch the children in your setting at play you may observe clear gender preferences in terms of what the boys and girls play with, who they play with and how they play. But because these gender preferences have already started developing does not mean that workers should be content to let them continue. Ways need to be found to allow those children who wish to explore alternative ways of playing and acting to do so. Certainly workers need to be aware of their own attitudes to gender and to watch carefully the models they offer and the language they use.

You may like to think about the contradiction implied when we say that children are active learners and when we say that children are socialised, at a very early age, into gender-specific roles. It is important to always think of the individual child with regard to the social context within which that child learns and develops. **Walkerdine et al.** (1989) and **Davies** (1989) both see individuals as being both complex and multiple, and say that every individual constantly creates and recreates themselves through the different experiences, situations, interactions and discourses they encounter. This is a hopeful view and one that suggests that we should not describe girls as always being 'passive', for example. Girls may be passive in certain situations or with certain people, but if we allow ourselves to see them as 'complex and multiple', we will see that, in their play, they are often engaged in sorting out a power struggle with boys. They are acting out the power relationships they have observed and often challenging them. Just watch the girls in your home corner to see how powerful they can be.

The argument goes that simply providing things to attract girls to the construction area or boys to the home corner is not enough. What researchers suggest is that those working with young children need to pay close attention to the struggle children go through in their play and talk as they construct their own identities and learn who they are and where they are positioned. Through adult role-modelling, the use of drama and story and through positive intervention, both boys and girls can be gently challenged and powerfully supported as they come to an understanding of who they want to be.

'RACE'

Historically, in Western Europe in particular, there has been a view that one race of people is genetically superior to another. This culminated, as you will know, in the extermination of six million Jews under Hitler's Nazi regime. Genocide and 'ethnic cleansing' continue to be tragic events as we approach the end of this century. In Britain the many groups of people who have come in from other countries have encountered active discrimination and prejudice: they have been encouraged to lose their cultures and languages in order to be assimilated into the host culture; they have been fêted and treated as 'exotic' in some attempts at multiculturalism. **Siraj-Blatchford** (1994) argues that the only acceptable approach for those working with young children and their families is one which is genuinely anti-racist and one which is prepared to examine racial inequality on an institutional and on a personal level.

The colour of a person's skin is significant. It is not something that can be ignored or glossed over. Not all children are the same and it is deeply insulting to treat all children as though they were. Very young children are aware of difference and it is important that they have the opportunity to express their observations about difference and to come to an understanding that difference is something to celebrate and not something to jeer at or ignore. Young children, in coming to define their own identity, are inevitably influenced by other people's perceptions of them. If you are white and part of the white majority, your whiteness is not something you are acutely aware of. But if you are black and part of a black minority, your very blackness is part of what defines you.

Offering a curriculum which is multicultural is a start, but it does not go far enough if you are genuinely concerned to ensure equality of access and opportunity. What is required is ensuring that the community you create within your setting is one in which children can pursue their discovery of concepts of fairness and justice. **Paley** (1995) showed that young children are passionate enquirers and that their fears relate primarily to things like being left out, feeling inadequate and being unfairly treated. Paley suggests that through story (and by story she means the acting out of real or imaginary situations through play and talk) children can address these very deep concerns and come to very real understandings.

RAINBOW PLAYGROUP'S EQUAL OPPORTUNITIES POLICY

You are now invited to read Rainbow Playgroup's Equal Opportunities Policy. As you do so please remember that, for the staff, the process of agreeing the policy was more important than the policy itself. Also remember that a policy as a piece of paper is worthless. It is the implementation and continual review of the policy which gives it life and meaning.

Rainbow Playgroup
Equal Opportunities Policy

Introduction

This policy was written after an intense programme of in-service training involving all the staff. The programme included a series of workshops where we as staff addressed our own attitudes and also where invited speakers came in to join us. We also examined the resources we have and the ways in which we use language ourselves. The first draft of the policy was shared with parents, many of whom offered their comments and criticisms. The whole process took a year and was, for all of us, a profoundly challenging and important experience.

Aims

1 We aim to ensure that we create an environment which is visually and emotionally welcoming to all children and their parents.
2 We aim to offer a range of learning opportunities which allow all children to build on what they already know.
3 We aim to promote talking and language (including the languages spoken by the children) throughout all activities.
4 We aim to ensure that the resources we offer are free of stereotypes and bias.
5 We aim to promote self-respect and respect for others through our own attitudes to the children, their parents and one another.

---

6 We aim to promote cooperation and collaboration rather than competition.

7 We aim to ensure that we are alert to any signs of discrimination and that we, as a staff group, do not ignore incidents which may be construed as discriminatory to any child or adult.

Operating the policy

1 The playgroup shall be organised in such a way that the commitment of all staff to a policy of equal opportunities is evident.

2 Staff will plan for and monitor all activities to ensure that no child is denied access to any activity on offer.

3 Resources, reflecting all aspects of the community we serve, will ensure that children and parents encounter books, scripts, artefacts and aspects of their home experience within the playgroup.

4 Parents will be invited to contribute their own skills, expertise and experience (where they are able) to ensure that their views become part of the views of the playgroup.

5 New parents will have the policy explained to them.

6 An awareness of equal opportunities will underpin all our future planning.

7 Our settling in procedures will include attempting to involve existing parents or older siblings where parents do not speak English.

8 Staff will not allow any racist or sexist incidence to pass unchallenged.

NOTE: This policy will be reviewed every year. Any parent/care giver who wishes to contribute their views about how the policy is operating is welcome to do so. There is a 'comments' box in the entrance hall. Parents/care givers may remain anonymous if they wish to do so.

CHILDREN WITH SPECIAL EDUCATIONAL NEEDS

Do you have children with special educational needs in your setting? How do you know that these children have special educational needs? Do you know what these particular needs are? Do you know what your responsibility is in dealing with these children?

In your setting you will have children whose development varies enormously. You may have a very tall four year old whose language development does not seem equivalent to that of other four year olds. You may have a tiny four year old who is extremely articulate, but who has difficulty with fine motor control. Children, as we know, vary enormously in their rate of development and in our zeal to describe children we sometimes label children as having 'special needs' or as being 'slow', 'naughty' or 'average'. Labels such as these suggest that we know something impossible – namely that there is such a thing as 'average' or 'normal'. More importantly, these labels are usually negative and not very informative or precise and, what is more, they often become attached to the child. A child who is labelled at an early age as being a failure in some way carries the additional disadvantage of having to overcome this label.

At the other extreme, however, is the fact that the early detection of particular difficulties allows for early intervention. This means that you, working with young children, are in a position to be alert to signs of problems that young children may be having (perhaps only temporarily) and know how to respond to these.

This is a tremendous responsibility, but the law now provides a framework to help all those involved in some way with the education of children under the age of five to know what to do. The 1993 Education Act introduced a Code of Practice on the Identification and Assessment of Special Educational Need which lays out five stages leading up to the formal assessment and statement of those children identified as having special educational needs. The ways in which the process is carried out are left to the school or setting, but each must have a statement which is published and available to parents and managers or governors and each is required to have a nominated member of staff with special responsibility for special needs. This person, sometimes called the Special Educational Needs Coordinator, or SENCO, must keep a register of all children with special needs and a record of what has been done to meet these needs.

To help you, here is an outline of the five steps set out in the Code of Practice:

Stage 1

This is the initial stage of gathering information and making some assessment of what the particular difficulty is. This is often initiated as the result of a parent, carer or worker expressing some concern about the child's development and is likely to be the stage most of you would be concerned with. It is important at this stage to liaise very closely with parents and to record in detail what the concern is, what steps have been taken and what the results are. It is recommended that workers, often together with parents, set targets for the child's progress and that these targets are also recorded. Other professionals may be involved at this stage – people like health visitors, speech therapists and so on. It is also recommended that reviews should be carried out, usually within a six-month period, and that if, after two such reviews, progress is not regarded as satisfactory (that is targets have not been met) Stage 2 is reached.

Stage 2

This is the point at which you feel you need additional specialist advice from people like doctors, specialist teachers for children with hearing or visual impairments and so on. In this stage you are asked to draw up an Individual Educational Plan (IEP) for the child and this should include:

- the nature of the child's difficulties;
- any special provision given and by whom; any particular programmes followed;
- what help the parents give;
- targets to be achieved by particular dates;
- any medical arrangements or pastoral care;
- the arrangements for monitoring and assessment;
- the arrangements for review of progress.

Again, parents need to be kept fully informed and involved and their views should always be taken into account.

Stage 3

During this stage the school or setting can call on additional professional help from people such as educational psychologists and the responsibility for the child is now shared with any outside agencies called in. A new IEP is drawn up and, again, partnership with parents is essential. If, on review, progress is not satisfactory the child may be referred to the local education authority for a statutory assessment. The setting or school must provide written evidence of all that has been done during stages 1 to 3.

Stage 4

The local education authority is required to carry out a statutory assessment of the child within 26 weeks of a request to do so by a parent, a worker, a school or an outside agency. This is the point where the school or setting feels unable to promote the child's development within the school or setting.

Stage 5

This is where a formal statement of the child's special educational needs is drawn up by the local education authority once it has established that the child's difficulties are:

- significant and/or complex;
- have not been met by the measures taken by the school or setting or support services;
- may call for resources which are not available within mainstream education.

You will see that this carefully structured framework does offer some support for workers attempting to both identify and cater for the needs of children.

Summing it up

- Avoid labelling children.
- Be aware of the Code of Practice.
- Publish your policy on how your setting identifies children with special educational needs and sets about attempting to meet these.
- Identify a member of staff who will take particular responsibility for this area.
- Liaise closely with parents and deal sensitively with them.

WORKING TOWARDS EQUITY AND EQUALITY

In this chapter we have started to examine the responsibility that all those working with young children have – morally, professionally and legally – to address issues of equality and equity for all children. This is an area that many workers find difficult to deal with because it sometimes forces them to face issues concerning their own view, beliefs and values. We all like to believe that we are without prejudice, yet confronting our innermost feelings sometimes reveals surprising and damaging things.

Within your setting you need to remember that you are empowered to create your own community. This community is bound to be influenced by the pressures and demands of the wider society, but it is possible to create a community which is socially just. You are in a position to influence the development of young children as social beings, initially within the social community of the setting or classroom, but equipping them to later look for justice in the wider community.

In all probability you will already have started doing some things towards achieving this goal. You may have looked at your resources in order to ensure that the images they offer are not stereotypes but show males and females and people from different cultures doing everyday, ordinary things. Images like this will allow the children both to build on their previous experience and to develop a sense of identity which they can be proud of. You will probably have thought about how you can support children whose first language is not English both in continuing to use that language, but also to acquire English.

You may have thought of providing books in languages other than English; of using story props to allow children into the meaning of the stories you tell and read; of displaying the alphabets and scripts used by the children and their families. You may have paid some attention to things like gender equality by considering what resources you offer in the home corner to encourage boys to play there; how you encourage girls to take active roles in outdoor play and block and construction play. You may have started to work closely with parents in order that you are able to understand their views and explain yours.

These aspects of ensuring equity and equality are important, but, in a sense, they are the ones that are relatively easy to do. In order that your policy has some 'teeth', however, there are some difficult things you have to do – and since these often involve changing attitudes, they take a long time. At William Patten Infants School in Hackney in the early 1980s the staff set about developing an anti-racist policy. After much debate and heart-searching, it was decided that the starting point had to be with the views of the staff. The staff split into two groups and each group met separately under the leadership of one of the teachers. The reason for the split was that those members of staff who were not teachers felt intimidated by the teachers and requested meeting on their own. Each group met regularly over a long period of time and the purpose was for each person, in turn, to relate their life story. There was only one rule – and that was that everyone had to listen and no one was allowed to interrupt. The point of doing this was for people who had previously been somewhat suspicious of those coming from a different cultural background to discover the things they had in common and to begin to develop an understanding of oppression.

So addressing issues of equality involves an examination of your own attitudes and also a willingness to consider factors of power and control that operate at a level beyond that of the individual. **Weiner** (1985) talks of the ongoing battle for power that exists between different groups – between men and women, between black and white people, between poor and rich. Inevitably, when considering such factors, one has to adopt a stance which is essentially political – and many people find this difficult.

But workers have an obligation to treat children as human beings and to deal with them seriously. In essence, anyone involved with young children, who are trying to understand the world and all its complexities, owes them the following:

- The presence of adults who are prepared to look objectively at their own practice to see how it affects different groups of children.
- A curriculum that values a range of cultures, languages and lifestyles.
- The provision of learning activities which allow children to explore ideas and concepts which will allow them to come to understand racism and other forms of oppression (**Kidner**, 1988).

REFERENCES

Anning, A., *The First Years at School*, Open University Press, 1991.

Bernstein, B., *Class, Codes and Control*, Routledge and Kegan Paul, 1974.

David, T., *Under Five – Under Educated*, Open University Press, 1990.

Davies, B., *Frogs and Snails and Feminist Tales*, Allen and Unwin, 1989.

DfEE, *Code of Practice on the Identification and Assessment of Special Educational Needs*, 1996.

Kidner, J., 'Under Fives' in Cohen, A. and Cohen, I. (eds), *Early Education: The Pre-school Years*, PCP, 1988.

Long, P., 'Special Educational Needs' in Robson, S. and Smedley, S. (eds), *Education in Early Childhood*, David Fulton Publishers, 1996.

MacGilchrist, B., *Managing Access and Entitlement in Primary Education*, Trentham Books, 1992.

Paley, V.G., *Kwanzaa and Me. A Teacher's Story*, Harvard University Press, 1995.

Siraj-Blatchford, I., *The Early Years: Laying the Foundations for Racial Equality*, Trentham Books, 1994.

Smedley, S., 'Working for Equality and Equity' in Robson, S. and Smedley, S. (eds), *Education in Early Childhood*, David Fulton Publishers, 1996.

Tizard, B. and Hughes, M., *Young Children Learning*, Fontana, 1984.

Walkerdine, V. and Girls from the Mathematics Unit, *Counting Girls Out*, Virago, 1989.

Weiner, G., *Just a Bunch of Girls*, Open University Press, 1985.

Weis, D. and Worobey, J., 'Sex Roles and Family Scripts' in Early Childhood in *Early Child Development and Care*, 77, 1991.

Wells, G., *The Meaning Makers*, Hodder and Stoughton, 1986.

8

DOCUMENTING WHAT
CHILDREN DO

We have talked earlier in this book about the importance of paying close attention to what children are doing in order that a programme of learning can be planned. In this chapter we look in more detail at how you can document children's progress – primarily for your own professional needs, but also to meet the requirements outlined in 'The Next Steps'.

OBSERVATION

Drummond (1993) says:

> 'The responsibility to assess, to watch and to understand learning is an awesome one; but the exercise of this responsibility is the only real fulfilment that teachers can know.'

You might want to read through that quotation and consider whether you agree with it or not.

Think about what you do everyday in your setting as you watch children play. You watch the children carefully, taking note of what they are doing. Then, having trained yourself, you attempt to interpret what you see. The observation you have made will probably have raised some questions in your mind. The answers to these questions not only help you to understand more about the children, but also give you an insight into how well you, the adult, are managing to support and extend children's learning. So, as Drummond puts it, you gain professional fulfilment in this way.

We observe children carefully in order to get a better understanding of what children already know and can do. This helps us plan what we might offer next in order to consolidate or extend learning. We also observe children in order to review our provision. Are we offering an environment which is broad, balanced, deep and challenging? Are all children given equal access to the curriculum and to our time?

Drummond (1994) says that observing children's learning is one of the most vital responsibilities of those who care for and educate children. When we observe children's amazing capacity for learning and development, it shows how much we must do in order to support, enrich and extend that learning. She goes on to say:

'Observing learning, getting close to children's minds and children's feelings, is part of our daily work in striving for quality. What we see, when we look closely, helps us to shape the present, the daily experiences of young children in all forms of early years provision. The act of observation is central to the continuous process of evaluation, as we look at what we provide and ask: is it good enough? Our careful observations of children's learning can help us make this provision better. We can use what we see to identify the strengths and weaknesses, gaps and inconsistencies, in what we provide. We can identify significant moments in a child's learning, and we can build on what we see.'

All those working with young children need to be involved in the observation and assessment process. If you operate a keyworker system, you will be primarily responsible for observing your key children. But in reality, in most settings, children move around so frequently that a worker may observe something very significant about a child who is not one of his or her key children. How you organise to observe children will be up to you as a staff group. There is no right way, but there are ways which are more efficient than others. Here are some examples:

In our playgroup each worker chooses to look at four children over the week. She tries to observe those children in different activities and jots down notes as she does so. Then, on Friday, when the children have gone home we all sit down and summarise what we have seen about each of the children. If another worker has observed one of the target children doing something interesting she will add her comments.

We vary what we do. At the moment we are observing the children in different areas. So my area this week is the home corner and I jot down notes about significant things that happen. Then we get together and share our observations.

We've tried everything! At one point we seemed to spend our whole time writing and decided that that was not the best use of our time. At the moment we have organised the room so that in each area there are clipboards with pens attached, so that if something significant

116

happens we can record it. But we each take responsibility for observing three children per week.

Observation is time-consuming and demanding. Some workers found it difficult at first because they were worried about their handwriting or their spelling. But we managed to persuade them that observation notes were working notes and would not be seen by parents. We also decided that we had to be selective about what we noted and that we didn't have to write long sentences in perfect English. Most of our comments are brief – sometimes just a couple of words. Something like 'counted to two' or 'played with Emma'. But where we have concerns about a child we tend to try and do a more in-depth observation. And we also try and do an in-depth observation soon after the child has settled and then, for each child, perhaps one per term.

All these workers are finding ways that suit them of observing and recording their findings. As you can see there is a great deal of trial and error involved as workers try and find what meets their needs. But a key point emerges and that is the question of what makes something a significant event.

You might like to stop and think about a child you have worked with and recall one moment which struck you as significant.

If you think about your own children's development or the development of children you know well, the obvious things are the so-called 'milestones' – the first word, the first step and so on. In terms of monitoring the development of the children in your care, you are looking for evidence of the child having moved on, having taken the next step in learning and development. Here are some examples:

Paolo was very shy and withdrawn. I felt it was significant when I saw him approach another child, tug his arm and point to the car he was holding.

Mariam was very unsettled at first, speaking no English. I felt it was significant when she stopped crying and joined in the play.

Boris never ever chose to look at books. It was significant when he came in one morning and headed straight for the book corner.

For Emilia, a significant moment was when she recognised her name in a Big Book we had made.

117

It was significant when Josepha wrote the letter J in her made up writing.

What to do with your observations

The first and most obvious thing you do with your observations is use them to plan what to offer next. In this way you are basing your planned programme on the interests and needs of the children as you have observed them. So observation informs planning. You will remember how we talked in the last chapter about how planning based on the observed interests and needs of individual children ensures that the programme provided offers genuine equality of access and opportunity to all children.

Once you have used your observations to plan what to offer next you can also think about how to use them to build a record of the child's progress over time. Inevitably, if all members of staff are keeping notes on what they notice, you will gather a veritable mountain of paper over the days and weeks. It is here that you need to use your judgement about what is significant. I would suggest that each keyworker be responsible for collecting together the bits of paper relating to her key children. She then needs to sift through them, extracting what is significant and discarding the rest. There is absolutely no point in keeping every observation note made. What you want to do is track each child's progress and the best way of doing this is to chart leaps in learning.

The other thing that each keyworker needs to do is ensure that she has observation notes covering all aspects of the curriculum. Where you have been worried about a child's emotional development it is natural that your observation notes will reflect this. But the child's overall development needs to be charted and you need to ensure that you have noticed something about the child's learning across the curriculum. In terms of 'The Desirable Outcomes' you will want to ensure that you have some observation notes and comments on all six areas of learning.

INTERPRETING WHAT YOU SEE

Writing down what you see and hear is easy enough. It is like taking a photograph. You record exactly what happens. But, as we have said earlier, observations on their own are of little use. What you need to do is interpret what you see and hear to understand what it shows you about the child's learning and development.

Let us look at some examples:

Four-year-old Abdul has recently arrived in the country from Bangladesh and does not yet have any English. You notice that he likes

118

to go into the book corner and sort out all the books according to size.

What does this tell you about his current interests? What does it suggest that he is paying attention to? And what might you introduce next to take this interest forward?

Did you think about bringing in some boxes of different sizes, inviting him to sort the books, by size, into the boxes? Did you think of reading the story – and using props to make it come alive for Abdul – of Goldilocks and The Three Bears? Did you think about introducing objects of varying sizes in the home corner as a follow-up to this – three different sized beds, three different sized teddies, three different sized bowls and so on?

> Four-year-old Amy loves books. She knows many of the books in the playgroup by heart and often chooses to look at books. One day you notice that she is actually drawing her finger under the text as she reads and that her retelling of the story is very close to the text.

What do you think she already knows? What do you think she is paying attention to? If you feel she is paying attention to print, what might you plan next to help her take the next step?

Drummond cites the example of a four-year-old girl who examines shells and pebbles under several different types of magnifiers. She spends a long time bringing the lens close to her eye and then moving it away again. She then picks up a shell, examines it under the magnifier on a tripod and then holds it to each ear in turn. Then she puts the shell again under the tripod, but this time places her ear, rather than her eye, against the magnifying glass as though she were trying to magnify the sound. Drummond asks:

> 'Whatever was she doing? Was she ignorant? Or stupid? No, neither of these. As I watched I realised she was asking a question, not out loud, but privately, to herself. She had established that the magnifying glass made the shell look bigger, now she wanted to know "will it make it louder?"'

Close observation allows us to make guesses about what children already know and about what their current interests are. We make our guesses in light of what we already know about that particular child and also what we know about how young children learn. So we use what we see and hear as the information we gather and then interpret this in light of our knowledge to help us plan what we will offer next to take learning forward.

119

BUILDING UP A PROFILE

One of the best ways of keeping track of children's progress is to start a profile for each child. This can be in the form of a file or notebook for each child and in this profile you can place some vital information.

Profiling can be defined as the process of assessing, recording and gathering evidence of children's progress and achievement over time. This ongoing process of evaluating progress is what is called 'formative assessment', and ideally a profile should include information gathered about the child from the child him- or herself (where possible), from the parents and from all the workers involved with the child.

A profile might include the following:

- some examples or samples of children's work;
- some comments written by workers about children's progress;
- some attempt by workers to analyse children's work and progress;
- comments from parents about the child's interests at home and about the child's progress in the setting;
- any comments the child might have made which show evidence of the child reflecting on his or her learning.

To illustrate this, here is an extract from the profile for four-year-old Farida:

a) samples of work plus comments of adults

On the day after her fourth birthday, Farida wrote her name in full and drew herself with a body, both for the first time. She also wrote the number four.

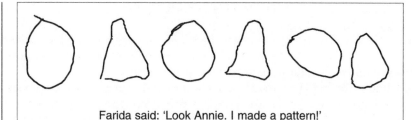

Farida said: 'Look Annie. I made a pattern!'

b) examples of workers' analysis of learning

29/4/96: Farida has come on in leaps and bounds. She spends a lot of time in the book corner and knows many of the books by heart. She can now retell a story, and turns the pages, using the pictures to help her. She is writing her name and is just starting to talk about letters. She spends a lot of time painting, drawing and making things. In the workshop area this week she made a box for her mother – choosing materials carefully and then decorated it with elaborate patterns of objects stuck to the surface.

c) parent's comments

I am happy with how Farida is getting on. She likes the playgroup and is looking forward to going to school. At home she looks at books a lot and sings lots of songs. She also likes to write.

d) child's comments

'Look, Annie. I made a pattern': Farida knew what a pattern was.
'Annie, I can write my name and my brother's name now. It goes F A R O U K – like this!': Farida knows what she can write and is proud of her achievements.

Profiling is time consuming, but you can see that a real picture of the child emerges from this. If you think about how much information a parent or teacher can get from such a profile you will realise that the amount of work is justified. But a word of warning! Please limit the amount of information you put into the profile. You need to learn to be selective and only include things that add to what you already know about the child. Don't, for example, include two samples of writing unless the second shows some way in which the child's writing has developed. And do remember to date all samples and comments and to always say why something has been included.

INVOLVING PARENTS

It is a cliché to say that parents know more about their own child than anyone else, but like most clichés it is true. Workers and teachers do, of course, get to know children well, but it is important to recognise that their knowledge of the child is limited. The person who sees the child in every situation at every time of the day and year is the parent. Parents are, indeed, experts when it comes to their own child. Despite this fact, many parents are made to feel that they know nothing and that their understanding of the child may be flawed or limited. This applies particularly to parents whose first language is not English or to parents who feel threatened by the education system and by authority. These parents find it difficult to have their voices heard and tend to adopt the stance that 'Teacher/playgroup workers know best!'

All parents, whatever their culture, language, background, social class or gender, care about their children. Parents who send young children to a nursery or créche or playgroup do so for many reasons: some because they feel their children will benefit from contact with other children; some because they want their children to have a head start in the education stakes; some because they need or want to work or study. But all parents want the best for their children and all parents deserve to be kept informed about how their children are making progress.

In the Italian nurseries, described in an earlier chapter, a great deal of work goes into keeping parents informed about their children's progress. Each child has a plastic wallet up on the wall and staff put into these brief comments about what the child has done that day. For parents of very young children, this information makes them feel involved in their children's progress. No parent wants to miss their own child's first step or first word. Parents of older children are equally entitled to learn of their children's progress. What is more, they will notice changes in their child's behaviour and learning at home and can add these to the child's profile.

Involving parents in this process is sometimes difficult and always requires that workers be sensitive and supportive in their approach. Most nurseries and playgroups collect information from parents when the child starts in the nursery. This will often include practical details, but some nurseries now invite parents to say something about their child's interests, fears, passions, likes and dislikes. This gives workers some starting point on which to base their assessment of progress. After all, all children starting in the nursery or playgroup come with a history. No child arrives as a blank slate. You can only assess progress against some starting point.

This involvement of parents is a good starting point, but a partnership with parents needs to go further than this. Many nurseries and playgroups now invite parents to become involved in contributing to the child's profile. Parents are invited to read through the profile and add their comments. You will, of course, need to think carefully about how you can manage this process in a way that allows those parents who have English as an additional language to have equal access to the partnership.

SUMMATIVE ASSESSMENT

The type of assessment we have been looking at is known as formative assessment. It is what you do all the time in your work both in order to ensure that the children are making progress and that what you are offering is providing the necessary challenge and support to ensure that this happens. Formative assessment is crucial to any educational enterprise.

Summative assessment is the type of assessment that summarises a child's achievements at a particular point in time. The most obvious example of summative assessment is the end-of-year report. You will remember from your own school days how getting the school report could either have been an occasion for celebration or one for misery. School reports used to consist, often, of a mark or grade accompanied by a very brief and bald comment – something like 'Judy has done very well at PE this term' or 'Marcus needs to try harder'. These comments gave parents no indication of exactly what the child had achieved over the year. Nor did it give any indication of what particular problems might be – nor any recommended course of action.

Nowadays summative assessments are better in that they do try and summarise all that workers or teachers have found from their formative assessments over a period of time. If you look back to the profiles, you can see how the worker could, at the end of a term or a year, make some comments summarising the child's progress in all areas of learning.

Here is an example:

Personal and social development: Farida started the year very timidly. She tended to play alone and was often observed to be withdrawn. Over the years, as her fluency in English developed, so did her confidence. She now comes to the playgroup with a smile, gets involved in all activities, plays alongside other children and has developed a particular friendship with Harinder. She is communicative and often takes the lead in play.

Language and literacy development: Farida knows many books and stories by heart. She can retell many stories – and her favourites are 'Peepo' and 'Brown Bear'. She knows many rhymes and songs and joins in enthusiastically. She can recognise her own name when it appears in books we have made and the names of some of her friends. She knows that, in English, books go from front to back and that print is read from left to right. She enjoys looking at books and making up stories.

She knows the difference between writing and drawing and will often choose to write letters, books, cards and fill in forms. She can write her own name and those of her brother and sister.

Mathematical development: Farida can count objects to 12 and recognises the symbols 1, 2, 3 and 4. She enjoys making patterns in her own drawing and in playing with blocks. She enjoys exploring space and has a wide vocabulary of words she both uses and understands – the names of shapes, words of position (like high), comparisons (like higher than) and superlatives (like highest). She often solves problems in her play that involve using mathematics.

Creative development: Farida enjoys choosing materials and tools to make things. She likes exploring colour and shape and enjoys painting, drawing, using clay and making things in the workshop area. She is very meticulous in her work and often spends a long time doing something. She enjoys singing and dancing and playing the musical instruments. She also enjoys playing different roles in the home corner and the outside play area and uses her imagination to good effect.

Physical development: Farida has overcome her initial nervousness and now enjoys playing outdoors on the climbing frame and large equipment. She can run, jump, balance, catch and throw. She uses a wide range of tools with great skill and manages fine tools like pens and pencils effectively.

Understanding of the world: Farida is interested in many things and often asks questions in her attempts to understand how things happen. She will often try things out and is willing to have a go and take risks. She knows a great deal about her own language and culture and will share this with other children and adults when she feels comfortable to do so.

You can see how a summative record like this gives some picture of the child's development over a period of time. A record like this sent to the child's primary school will give the receiving teacher some indication of what the child has already done and what the child's interests and strengths are. A teacher receiving Farida's report would be unlikely to assume that Farida knows nothing about reading and writing, for example. There is clear evidence of what she already knows and this provides the teacher with some indication of where to start her programme for this child.

Summing it up

Everyone involved in the education and care of young children has a professional obligation to document children's progress. This is a difficult task and one that many workers find daunting. It is important to remember that your setting needs to work out a policy on how this is to be done.

- The only way you can know how children are progressing is to observe them as they play and record your observations.
- Everyone involved with the child should contribute to this.
- The observation notes on their own are only of use if you analyse them to find what they show you about what the child already knows and can do, what the child is interested in or what the child is paying attention to.
- On the basis of this you can evaluate both the child's progress and how well you are meeting the child's needs.
- Observation then suggests what you should plan next in order that children can take the next step in their learning.
- Parents and children should be involved in the assessment process.
- One way of doing this is to build up profiles for each child in which workers carefully select examples of children's work (and these can include photographs of things the child has done), their own comments and evaluations, comments from children and from parents.
- Even very young children can contribute to their profiles. What you are looking for are examples of children reflecting on what they can do or what they have achieved.
- Parents are experts about their own children: their views on children's progress are essential.
- Parents should be invited, on entering the setting, to give information that includes details of the child's interests and experiences. This provides a baseline against which progress can be assessed.
- All parents need to be involved in this partnership and ways need to be found of involving those parents who, for one reason or another, may be reluctant or unable to contribute.
- A good programme of formative assessment can lead to summative assessment which carries information that is meaningful to parents and of use to receiving teachers or workers.
- It is time-consuming and difficult, but worth the effort!

REFERENCES

Ackers, J., '"Why involve me?" Encouraging Children and their Parents to Participate in the Assessment Process' in Abbott, L. and Ridger, R. (eds), *Quality Education in the Early Years*, Open University Press, 1994.

Bartholomew, L. and Bruce, T., *Getting to Know You: A Guide to Record Keeping in early Childhood Education and Care*, Hodder and Stoughton, 1994.

Devereux, J., 'What We See Depends on What We Look For: Observation as Part of Teaching and Learning in the Early Years' in Robson, S. and Smedley, S. (eds), *Education in Early Childhood*, David Fulton Publishers, 1996.

Drummond, M.J., *Assessing Children's Learning*, David Fulton Publishers, 1994.

Drummond, M.J., 'Observing Children' in Smidt, S. (ed.) *'I Seed it and I Feeled it': Young Children Learning*, UNL Press, 1995.

9

PARTNERSHIPS WITH PARENTS

In this chapter we explore the issue of how your setting can set up a partnership with parents which is more than a tokenist gesture, but one that recognises both the problems involved in partnerships and the advantages of them.

PARENTS AND SCHOOLS: A POTTED HISTORY

The role of parents with regard to the education of their children out of the home has a long and difficult history. There were those who held that teachers were professionals who knew best about what young children needed and that parents should be happy to hand over their young children without question into such capable hands. Home and school were kept separate with no recognition of the fact that learning begins at home and that parents are fundamentally involved in the education process.

When the importance of the role of parents began to be recognised it was in the sense that 'good' parents are able to help their children's learning by supporting what happens in the school or nursery. 'Bad' parents were seen to hold children back. For several decades it was believed that it was the role of schools and teachers to educate these 'inadequate' parents (who were invariably poor or black) and to compensate for the perceived inadequacies of the home. This view was exemplified in programmes like The Head Start programme in the USA. Even the Plowden Report in 1967, which advocated partnership with parents, saw the role of parents limited to that of raising funds and being informed about their children's progress and development by teachers through regular meetings. So parents continued to play a largely passive role – receiving information rather than contributing to children's progress. It is only in recent years that a different view of parents has emerged, and much of that has to do with the work of researchers like **Tizard and Hughes** (1984) and **Gordon Wells** (1986) who demonstrated effectively that most homes, regardless of socioeconomic level or other factors, provide rich learning environments. Alongside this has come a recognition that parents know more about their own children than teachers and playgroup workers do and if children are to be offered rich learning experiences in the nursery and playgroup which allow them to build on what they already know, this expertise of parents needs to be made accessible to all those working with the child.

The changing role of parents is reflected at the official level. Under the 1944 Education Act parents were seen as having a duty to ensure that their children received education suitable to their age and ability. The Taylor Report (1977) emphasised parental responsibility, but did recognise that individual parents might need to band together in order to have a collective voice. The report advocated that parents should have equal representation with teachers, the local education authority and the local community on school governing bodies. The 1980 Education Act, which followed this report, only partly implemented these recommendations and it was only with the 1986 Education (No 2) Act that parents were given equal representation with local education authority members. The Act further required that all schools furnish parents with an annual report and hold an annual meeting for parents.

But the most important piece of legislation recognising that parents have rights as well as responsibilities came in the early 1980s with the Warnock Report which looked at children with special needs. In this report teachers and schools were required to seek the full involvement of parents and the notion of parental/school partnerships really emerged.

In the late 1980s with the publication of the 1988 Education Act the role of parents shifted again, with the emphasis now being placed on parental choice. This notion of parental choice is a key theme underpinning much of current government legislation – as you will realise when you consider recent legislation regarding nursery education. It is exemplified in the Parents Charter (1994). This document suggests that parents can influence schools significantly through their right to choose schools for their children. It also suggests that parents become 'active partners with the school and its teachers'. This approach shifts education to a new arena – that of the market place – and places responsibilities on parents to exercise their rights as consumers.

You might like to consider this in depth and decide whether you feel that education is best situated in the market place and whether the concept of parents as consumers is the best way forward in establishing good relationships.

You can see from this how parents, over the past 20 years, have been given some rights individually to be involved with the education of their children and some collective rights in terms of serving on governing bodies, which now have increased powers.

WHY INVOLVE PARENTS?

Nowadays it is rare to find anybody who doesn't think that parental involvement in education is a 'good' thing. But defining quite why this is so is complex. Here are some suggestions, drawn from **Robson** (1996):

Parents have rights and schools and settings need to be accountable to parents. The Children Act (1989) states that all parents have responsibilities toward their own children and these include concern for their care and education. More importantly, however, is the fact that parents are their child's first educators and have a continuing concern for their child's education away from the home. This view enshrines the rights of all parents to be consulted and informed about their child's progress and makes institutions involved in the care and education of children accountable to parents.

Parents can have a positive effect on their children's attainment and progress. **Tizard et al.** (1988) showed that 97 per cent of parents of children in the reception class helped them at home with reading. They had similar findings with regard to parents helping their children with mathematics. A number of schemes for involving parents more directly with their children's work in schools have revealed gains. Working-class parents are as keen and able to help their children with learning at home as more middle-class parents. The fact that all parents want their children to do well at nursery and school has important implications for how workers relate to parents.

Parental involvement in the school can help minimise conflicts between the values of home and school. We have touched on this in earlier chapters. Since all schools and settings serve diverse communities with different value systems the more that is known about these values and beliefs the better the relationship between parents and workers. Where workers are able to understand and consider different styles and expectations they are more likely to be able to arrive at a shared and common way of approaching both care and education.

Parental involvement in the school can have positive spin-off effects for parents themselves. Where parents are invited to become actively involved in the life of the nursery they gain insights into what it is the workers are doing and why. So where a school or setting takes time and trouble to explain to parents the reasons for providing play opportunities or why reading to children is important, for example, parents themselves learn and may be able to implement some of what they have learned at home.

Parental involvement in the school can have positive spin-off effects for teachers and workers. Where parents are actively involved in the nursery workers have the opportunity to learn more about the parent and child, about the values and principles operating within the child's life out of the setting. Since one of the underpinning principles of high-quality early learning is building on what children already know and can do, the more that is known about the child's life in all its aspects the better the provision within the nursery or setting is likely to be.

Parents can offer workers and teachers support. Where partnerships with parents are established the support of parents can be a powerful tool when change and improvement is sought. There are many examples of parents taking action in order to ensure that a playgroup acquires better premises or in supporting workers' requests for better pay and conditions.

The implications of this for settings

It is clear from this that establishing a close and respectful attitude between parents and workers is crucial to the well-being of the children. Research shows that all parents, regardless of class or cultural group or social position, want what is best for their children. All parents are keen to help their children and many will give up a great deal to see their children succeed.

One of the difficulties, however, is that there are parents who do not know the best way in which to do this and who lack the confidence to approach staff. There are also many parents who have a limited command of English and who are often dependent on getting a second-hand version through translation. These may be very real barriers to establishing partnerships and are issues that are certainly worth addressing.

Another very real barrier may be the attitude of staff to parents. Where parents are perceived as being 'too pushy' or 'not interested', establishing relationships can be difficult. It is worthwhile examining your own attitudes to the parents of the children in your setting and seeing if you can honestly define parents who make you uncomfortable for one reason or another.

Try to work out what it is that makes you uncomfortable and think of ways in which you can overcome your prejudice.

Here is what Martha, a worker at a playgroup said:

'I realised that Tommy's mother made me feel very uncomfortable. She is a teacher and very confident. Every day she would come in and ask what Tommy had done that day. I always felt that she was critical, although she never actually said anything critical. I used to dread open evenings. Then the organiser of the playgroup sug- gested that we had some social occasions for parents where we invited a small group of parents in to talk about their expectations for their children. We tried to plan groups that were very mixed and in the group with Tommy's mother was a mother who speaks Turkish, a single parent and a very young mother. I started by telling them what we were planning and what our aims were and then asked for their comments. I was really surprised when Tommy's mother said that she was hoping that Tommy would develop his self-confidence and his independence and his ability to get on with children of his own age. She said she was very happy with his progress at the playgroup and she reassured the very young mother, whose child had only just joined. And she was really nice to the Turkish mother and showed her pictures of what the children had been doing. I had to revise my opinion of her!'

HOW TO INVOLVE PARENTS AS EQUAL PARTNERS

There are many things you can do to make parents feel that the setting the child attends 'belongs' to them. And you will find that there are many things that you already do.

Home visiting

It is recognised that moving away from home for the first time is traumatic for both child and parent. Many schools and nurseries try to reduce the level of stress by visiting the child and parent at home before the child actually starts in the setting. The obvious advantage of this is that the initial contact takes place in a situation which is familiar and where the parent is in control. But this is a sensitive area and there may well be parents who do not want to be visited at home – particularly where the parent is living in temporary accommodation or where the parent sees the visit as a way of outsiders assessing the 'quality' of the home and of the parents. The rights of parents to refuse a visit should be respected and it is important that the school or setting is clear about the purpose of the visit and able to explain this to parents.

Here is how one nursery teacher sees the purpose of home visits:

'It is our policy that each child gets this opportunity to meet me in the safety of her/his home environment. . . . I usually take a puzzle, a book, some drawing material and a photo book with pictures of the team, the school, our class, and the children at work. We look through this book together, often with grandparents, aunts and uncles, as well as parents and the child and siblings. I chat a bit about the kinds of things children can do in our class. The pictures speak for themselves when I am unable to communicate in the

131

family's language. That, and a great deal of body language, smiles, gestures usually gets the message across.

During the visit I also take some photographs of the child. They are used later when the child comes to school to make her/his space on the coat hooks, the towel hook and the third, a whole body one, for the magnet board. The home visit is a good opportunity to ask the parents to write their child's name in the family's language. . . . From there I can enlarge it on the photocopier at school and use it in our graphics area and anywhere else where the child's name appears in English.'

(Voss, 1995)

Visiting the nursery or setting

All children and their parents should visit the setting prior to the child start-ing. You may want to think about sending an individual invitation to the child and parent, making the visit something special. Many settings find that allowing parents and children to visit as often as possible eases the child's entry to the setting and makes the parent feel more comfortable. It is impor-tant to try to ensure that not too many new children and parents visit at one time. The best way of making parents and children feel important and valued is to allow one member of staff (perhaps the keyworker) time to be able to talk to both parent and child. It is worth considering the point that these initial visits are going to be the time when the parent or carer forms her or his initial impression of the setting, so it is important that they are carefully planned for.

Settling in

Some children find the transition from visiting to attending the setting on a permanent basis easy: others – as you will well know – find it difficult. The child's distress will convey itself to the parent and this may damage the rela-tionship with the setting. You will want to consider your settling in arrange-ments with care. Most settings invite (indeed often insist) that parents stay with children at least for the first few days. You will want to think about how you handle this with parents who cannot manage because of work or domestic commitments. The presence of parent or carer is reassuring for the child and if you want parents or carers to be able to stay with the child you need to give them adequate notice of this. Most settings also advise parents to tell children when they are leaving and not just to disappear.

Staying in touch

Parents, leaving young children in the care of others, feel that they are missing out on significant moments in their child's development. You will have read in an earlier chapter how the nurseries in Reggio Emilia keep parents in touch with what their children have done each day. There are many different ways of doing this – from wall displays to link books that go between home and setting to informal chats at the start or the end of the day. In addition to this you will want to ensure that you arrange particular times when parents can come in and have an in-depth discussion about their child's progress. Do remember that the timing of this is important. If you have evening meetings there may be parents who will not attend. Similarly meetings during the day will exclude some parents. You need to work with parents to find out which is the best time for them and to do your best to meet this.

Involving parents in assessing progress

Parents need and should be involved in both commenting on what they observe about their child's progress and development at home and contributing to what workers observe about development within the setting. If you operate a profile system in your setting you will ensure that parents' voices are heard.

Involving parents in the day-to-day life of the setting

Many nurseries and playgroups invite parents in to help during the day. This help may vary from reading to children to cooking with them or accompanying them on outings and so on. However parents are involved, it is important that their role is clearly spelled out to them so that they know what it is they are doing and why. This implies that workers will have to talk to parents about what they are doing and why. This is one of the best ways of genuinely involving parents in the life of the nursery. You may invite a parent in for a specific purpose: perhaps a mother who has just had a new baby or a father who is a nurse. Again, an explanation of what you want them to do on this visit is important.

Home/school projects

Many settings try to find ways of offering parents things to do at home to build on what has happened in the nursery or setting during the week. Parents may be invited to take home books to read with children or to borrow toys from a toy library. An initial meeting with new parents to introduce the materials and explain ways in which they may be used is useful for parents who may feel reluctant to do things that they see as 'not their role'.

Offering learning opportunities to parents

Some nurseries place great emphasis on their role in educating parents. Some are able to offer parents classes ranging from what to do about temper tantrums or bed-wetting to classes in English as an additional language. This is, of course, very dependent on your resources, but if you have a spare room in your setting you might want to consider offering such classes.

ONE EXAMPLE OF SUCCESSFUL HOME–SCHOOL LIAISON

There have been a number of examples of educationalists involving parents in early literacy programmes in an attempt to promote children's acquisition of literacy. One of the best documented is the Sheffield Early Literacy Development Project, carried out between 1988 and 1990. This was a small-scale project, involving initially only 20 preschool children and their families, but the methodology of that study was taken up successfully by a number of later projects and there are certainly features of this project which point to more successful and focused home–school relationships.

The programme was built on the idea that all children encounter literacy events within their families and that all young children actively try to make meaning in their encounters with written language. From reading previous chapters you will realise that the researchers saw literacy as something that emerges through children's explorations of their world and their interactions with significant people in that world. Parents and other family members clearly play an important role in children's early attempts to make sense of what they encounter.

The project involved two elements we have touched on earlier in this chapter. The first was a series of home visits, and the second a series of meetings with parents. None of this sounds new, but the most significant feature of the project was that each visit and each meeting was carefully planned and evaluated. You might like to know that the project was one of 12 carried out in European Member States as part of the European Commission Action Research Programme in the Prevention of Illiteracy.

In the home visiting programme the aims were to introduce books and other resources for literacy, to model ways of using these with children and to share ideas about early literacy development with parents. The team of researchers was sensitive in its approach to parents and ensured that visits were made at times to suit parents. So although visits varied according to the needs of parents, each one had core features: a review of what parents and children had been doing since the last visit; some input in terms of books, writing materials and examples of environmental print; and a plan of what parents and children might do with the resources. Parents were asked to keep all examples of children's drawing and writing in a scrapbook and, where possible, to date each example and put a comment on this.

The meetings programme took place at the school and involved parents in attending five meetings. At the first meeting parents worked with their own child on literacy-related activities, but in subsequent meetings a crèche was organised for the children and the parents were then able to participate in discussions and workshops. The researchers faced the very real temptation of using their expertise to tell the parents things, but they were determined that the meetings should not involve a one-way transmission of information, but should seek to set up a dialogue with parents. So parents were invited to show each other their scrapbooks and to discuss their own observations of their children's progress. At the end of each meeting parents were given a handout summarising what had happened at the meeting and including illustrations and quotations from the families taking part.

The project was regarded as a success in that children's early literacy was clearly encouraged and that had been the original intention. But it was also successful in that it had benefits for the parents and for their attitudes to formal education. As a result of the project parents began to believe that they were regarded as vital in terms of their children's progress. After all, educationalists had taken time to visit them at home and had been prepared to time their visits to suit the parents. Educationalists had been prepared to talk to parents about how young children learn and had been eager to listen to what parents had to say. A genuine dialogue had been established and everyone had benefited as a result.

You can read more about the project in **Hannon, Weinberger and Nutbrown** (1991).

Summing it up

A great deal has been written about the importance of partnerships with parents and you can find some of the books and chapters in the list at the end of this chapter. Partnership with parents is fundamental to a successful learning environment for all children, but particularly for children in their first steps away from home.

- All parents want the very best for their children.
- All parents are crucial in the education and development of their own children.
- A partnership with parents, based on mutual respect, will benefit everyone concerned.
- Parents need to be made to feel that they are worth listening and talking to.
- Settings need to ensure that the environment is welcoming to all parents and that all parents know that successful education is a joint enterprise.
- The ways in which parents can become involved need to be clear and explicit.

- Parents' fears need to be acknowledged.
- Workers need to ensure that they are willing to give information, but equally willing to receive it.
- Settling in procedures need to be carefully considered and explained to parents.
- Settings need to decide how they will ensure that parents with little or no English are not disadvantaged.
- Sometimes having a theme based on the observed interests of the children allows settings to establish strong partnerships with parents, particularly where the theme selected provides opportunities for parents to contribute their own skills, their knowledge, their talents and their experience.

REFERENCES

Hannon, P. and Weinberger, I., 'Sharing Ideas about Pre-School Literacy with Parents' in Dombey, H. and Meek, M. (eds), *First Steps Together: Home–School Early Literacy in European Contexts*, Trentham Books, 1994.

Hannon, P., Weinberger, J. and Nutbrown, C., 'A Study of Work with Parents to Promote Early Literacy Development', *Research Papers in Education,* 6(2), 1991.

Robson, S., 'Home and School: A Potentially Powerful Partnership' in Robson, S. and Smedley, S. (eds), *Education in Early Childhood*, David Fulton Publishers, 1996.

Tizard, B. and Hughes, M., *Young Children Learning*, Fontana, 1984.

Tizard, B., Blatchford, B., Burke, J., Farquar, C. and Plewis, I. *Young Children at School in the Inner City*, Lawrence Erlbaum, 1988.

Voss, B., 'Supporting Young Children' in Smidt, S. (ed.), *'I Seed it and I Feeled it': Young Children Learning*, UNL Press, 1995.

Wells, G., *The Meaning Makers*, Hodder and Stoughton, 1986.

10

DOCUMENTING WHAT YOU DO FOR OTHERS

If you have read this book from the beginning, up to this point you have considered what is known about how young children learn best; you have looked at the 'Desirable Outcomes' and considered how best to promote and support children's learning across the six areas of learning; you have considered the importance of equality of opportunity and access for all children and for the adults working with them; and you have thought about how important it is to document what you and the children do as part of your own professional role.

The DfEE will be publishing documents to describe the new arrangements which will be put in place for paying nursery education grants. These documents will set out the conditions and requirements upon providers accepting certificates of eligibility and providers claiming nursery education grant from those local authorities who have in place an interim Early Years Development Plan for the Autumn term 1997 and the Spring term 1998. The documents will provide guidance to providers on the handling of certificates of eligibility. It is important to note that whilst the voucher scheme has been abolished, the 'Next Steps' continues to set out a comprehensive framework of good management practice which all settings could usefully adopt.

Starting with self-appraisal

Good management practice means knowing what your setting is able to offer now, evaluating this and deciding what might be done to improve the quality of care and education within your setting. No setting is perfect and there are always things that can be done to make improvements. You can only begin this process of improvement if you have carried out some sort of self-assessment or self-appraisal.

You will not be surprised then, to find that the first thing suggested in 'The Next Steps' as a starting point for good management practice is to carry out some sort of self-assessment. Self-assessment involves you in looking at your current practice, your staffing arrangements and a range of other things in order to assess your own current likelihood of being able to prepare children to meet the Desirable Outcomes on reaching statutory school age. Evaluating your own practice can be difficult and it is certainly something that needs to be done with sensitivity and something that must involve all staff. If the head or coordinator carries out the self-assessment unaided and merely fills in a form, the exercise becomes a paper exercise and one of little value to the setting. You should see this opportunity to review your provision – and to do this as honestly as you can – as a learning experience for you and your co-workers.

It is good management practice not only to review what you offer at present, but also to write down, or document, your findings so that you are able to produce some written evidence of what you do and what your policies are. You will, in any event, need to produce some documentation when your setting is inspected and it is a good idea to start doing this as soon as possible. Some settings, in a panic about the amount of paperwork involved in an inspection, tend to spend hours writing up fine-sounding policies and spend more time on doing this than on ensuring that the children's learning and development is fostered. You are not expected to produce dozens of fancy documents. Most of what you are asked to produce should, ideally, be in the form of working documents. After all, no policy can ever really be regarded as final, since you and your ideas will change over time. Policies need to reflect your thinking to date and be flexible enough to be changed when your thinking changes.

Here are some of the documents you will want to start producing (if you don't already have them) as part of your initial self-appraisal.

Information for parents

Most settings already produce some sort of booklet or prospectus for parents which tells them something about what the setting has to offer their children. Parents may find such booklets helpful when they are choosing between one setting and another; more importantly, producing such a booklet forces you to review what it is that you offer and why. How you produce this is entirely up to you and dependent on your means. Some settings have been able to produce very attractive and glossily produced booklets for parents. It is not essential that your booklet is expensively produced. What matters is what the booklet says and how accessible it is to parents.

- You will need to decide what information to put into the booklet. It is important that parents know what your *aims*, as a setting are, and you will want to refer to how you are preparing children to meet 'The Desirable Outcomes' when they start school.

- You might want to talk about your *curriculum*: how you ensure that children's learning is broad and balanced and that you offer children opportunities to learn through play in all six areas of learning.
- You will want to make a statement about your setting's arrangements for ensuring *equality of access and opportunity* for all children and perhaps talk about how you encourage boys and girls, monolingual and bilingual children and children with disabilities to partake fully of your programme.
- You might want to say something briefly about how you observe children and about how the involvement of parents in your *assessment* programme is vital. In fact, a section on how parents can become involved in the setting as *partners* is certainly something worth including.
- You will want to include some *basic information*: things like names of staff, opening hours and any particular rules you operate (things like 'No sweets' or 'No bullying').

Two additional points are worth making. The first is that you need to ensure that you write about your setting using language which is straightforward. Try and avoid using 'jargon' as much as you can. Write for parents just as you talk to them. The second point is that you need to think about how you can produce your booklet in more than one language if you have many parents for whom English is an additional language. And finally, remember that you have easy access to wonderful illustration. Use the children's drawings to make your booklet attractive and individual to your setting.

Special educational needs

This is an area where you do need to have a written policy statement in which you document exactly what your setting's policy is with regard to special educational needs, who monitors this and how your policy is implemented. For more details about this refer back to the chapter on ensuring equality of access and opportunity.

In your policy you need to address the following issues and questions:

- What is your policy on special educational needs?
- Is this policy agreed and known by all staff?
- How does your policy relate to the Code of Practice on the identification and assessment of special educational needs?
- Who takes responsibility within the centre for special educational needs?
- Do you offer Individual Education Plans (IEPs) for children identified as having special educational needs?
- What support are you able to offer children who have special needs?
- How do you involve parents in the process?
- How often are you able to review children's progress?
- How do you review your policy on SEN?

Equal opportunities

You will want to ensure that prospective parents and users of your setting understand that ensuring equality of opportunity is one of your underpinning aims. One way to do this is to have a clearly thought out and agreed policy on equality of opportunity. This policy needs to have been agreed and to be implemented by all members of staff and needs to be shared with parents.

Some settings choose to include this policy in their booklet for parents. Others display it prominently in the setting, so that it can be seen by all visitors and users. Still others publish a separate policy document or booklet which is given to all parents.

You will want the policy to show that you are aware of how some groups in society may be denied access and opportunity on the grounds of age, gender, ethnicity, race, language or a number of other factors. You will want to indicate that, within your setting, you will ensure that no child or parent is denied access to either the opportunities on offer nor to the time of the adults in the setting. You will want to address the following issues and questions:

- Who is responsible for ensuring that the policy is understood, implemented and reviewed?
- How have parents been involved in developing and maintaining the policy?
- How do you provide equality of opportunity for boys and girls?
- How do you provide equality of opportunity for children with languages other than English?
- How do you provide equality of opportunity for children with special educational needs?
- How do you provide equality of opportunity for black children?
- How do you monitor your provision and your resources?

The curriculum

You do need to have something in writing about the curriculum on offer for the children. This is a working document for all the staff in your setting and need not be produced in the same format as the booklet for parents – although that should obviously contain some condensed information about what you offer and why.

In this you want a statement of your educational aims. You may find it helpful to look back to earlier chapters in this book to help you with this.

You will want to address the following questions and issues as a staff group:

- Who is responsible for planning the day-to-day programme within your setting?
- Who is responsible for planning the longer term programme?

- How do you plan? (We are back to observations and how they should inform planning.)
- What would you say is your educational philosophy? In other words, how do you think young children learn best? What writers and researchers influence you in this?
- How do you ensure that you plan for learning in all six areas of the 'Desirable Outcomes'?
- How do you plan for learning indoors and out?
- How do you monitor and evaluate children's progress?
- How do you record your observations and evaluations?
- Do you use a profiling system?
- Do you involve parents in the process of assessment? How?
- How do you pass children's records or profiles onto the next setting the child attends?
- Do you carry out formative and summative assessment?
- Are all adults involved in the observation, planning and assessment cycle?

Staffing information

If you do not already have this information it is worth gathering it together in preparation for your initial inspection. You will want to have a list of the names of all staff members, the hours they work and the jobs they do. In addition you need to add details of the training and qualifications of staff members (things like Qualified Teacher Status, NNEB training, Pre-School Learning Alliance Training, etc.). Note down also how long each member of staff has been working in your setting.

You also need to know what the staff : pupil ratios are, and in particular, the ratio of adults to children aged four.

This basic information will be easy to gather. Less easy, but just as important, is some information about your own training programme – that is what you as a staff group do to take your own learning and understanding forward. To help you in considering this, here are some suggestions:

- Invite each member of staff to write down any training they have been involved in over the past two years. Staff may have attended courses as part of their own professional development; you may have had a staff training day on 'play' (for example); you may have invited in a speaker to talk to the staff. Anything relevant to the learning and development of young children should be included.
- Make a list of all the training events you have carried out within your own setting.
- Make a list of any books, videos or resources you have used or that have been recommended to you.

- Write a brief statement about how you, as a staff group, decide what training should be offered. Do you all just do your own thing, or do you follow a theme for the year or term – something like 'early numeracy' or 'emergent literacy' perhaps? Is there one member of staff who is responsible for planning staff development? How are you able to fund staff development? Do you set aside some of your budget and divide it up equally between all staff members, or do individuals just approach you for help, or do staff members have to fund their own training?

Management

Just as there is no one prescribed way of offering your curriculum, there is no one management style that will guarantee the quality of your provision. You may find it a useful exercise to reflect on just who takes responsibility for what and document this.

Here are some questions you will need to answer when compiling a brief statement on your management programme:

- Who is responsible for managing the day-to-day provision?
- Who is responsible for managing the budget?
- Who is responsible for keeping records of attendance?
- What are the chief aims and objectives of your setting?
- Who takes responsibility for ensuring that all members of staff are actually doing what they are supposed to do and that they are both efficient and effective? Do you operate any form of 'supervision' or 'performance review'?
- How do you organise your sessions?
- How do you ensure that four year olds have their understanding and their interests taken into account? (This leads into your observation and planning cycle.)
- How do you ensure that you provide opportunities for four year olds to work on their own and with others? What consideration do you give to cooperative play?
- How do you monitor whether your provision allows children to get deeply involved over long periods of time? (Again, using observation, but this time to monitor your provision.)
- How do you plan for both indoor and outdoor activity?
- How do you provide and use materials and equipment?
- How do you decide where adults are to be deployed?

Premises and equipment

Many of you will be working in premises that present difficulties since they were not designed to promote the learning and development of young children. It is recommended that you take a close look at your premises in order to assess their suitability. Here are some questions you might like to ask:

- How far do your premises support the learning and development of young children? Think about things like the available space indoors and out; how the space is utilised and is this the best possible way of doing this; are rooms set up to encourage children's independence or are there physical barriers which make free movement around your setting difficult for children?
- Take a close look at your resources and ask if they best meet the learning needs of the children in your care. Do you depend a great deal on work sheets or do the resources themselves invite children to solve problems and express ideas? Do the resources reflect the mix of children in the setting? Do you have sufficient numbers of things like books, blocks and so on? It is useful to list what resources you feel need extending or replacing and then, perhaps, to suggest an action plan for how funds may be raised to purchase these, together with some target dates. If you make use of local libraries or toy libraries make sure these appear in your statement. If you do not have access to outdoor space explain what you do to make up for this.
- Think about 'people resources' and how you are able to bring in outside people to support children's learning and development. You may involve parents on a regular basis, using their specific skills or knowledge or training them in your approach so that they can support ongoing learning. You may invite in theatre groups, musicians, puppet shows, people from the local community. Keep a list.
- Do staff and children have easy access to all the resources? This goes back to the question of how your resources are set out and whether you ensure that they are appropriately labelled in some way so that children can find what they want without being dependent on adults. Ideally, in a purpose-built nursery you will be able to arrange rooms on a semi-permanent basis, but for those of you sharing premises the issue of space and storage is often a difficult one. It is worth writing a simple statement about how you plan for setting up each day so that children and adults do, indeed, have easy access to resources and activities.

Documenting the difficulties you may have with premises will clarify your own position and give you something to present to inspectors when they visit your setting.

Children's welfare

In your setting you will ensure that you provide the most stimulating and supportive environment for all the children in your care. You may have children who, for one reason or another, need additional support and understanding, and will often already have made links with outside agencies involved in the lives of children. In considering how well your setting is able to promote children's welfare you might like to consider these questions:

- Are all staff aware of child protection procedures? Have you, as a staff group, agreed on the procedure to be followed within your setting where there is concern about a child's safety?
- Have you, as a staff group, agreed a policy on promoting 'good' behaviour? How do you ensure that all staff members and parents are consistent in applying this policy?
- Detail your arrangements for liaising with other agencies – doctors, nurses, social workers, health professionals, and any others involved in the well-being of the child in society.

SUMMING UP GOOD MANAGEMENT PRACTICE

The initial list of required documentation may look daunting at first, but once you check through it you will realise that you are well on the way to already having at least the information necessary to write brief outlines. You probably already have a booklet for parents and basic information about staff and what they do. The best advice is to work slowly towards gathering together the documentation and just having brief notes on areas you haven't yet addressed as a staff group. A policy is only of use where it has been discussed and agreed and is being implemented. So as long as you can show that you are aware of what is required and are working towards that you will be acting professionally.

ACTION PLANS

Following on from an inspection you will be required to write an action plan. This is a written outline of how you plan to improve some aspects of your provision within a given time – usually within 12 months after an inspection.

You cannot plan to improve everything at once, so you will need to focus on the key areas or issues for action which will be identified by the inspector and appear in your inspection report. Your action plan should state how you and your colleagues plan to address each of these issues. Your action plan should be clear and concise.

The purpose of an action plan is to force you to address key issues and consider ways of working together to improve your educational offer. An action plan allows you to recognise what you do well and helps you move towards a better inspection report next time you are inspected.

After your first inspection you receive a report which identifies key issues. Your first action plan, written in response to this, becomes the starting point of a long-term process of continuous evaluation and improvement in your setting. It is important that you see the writing of action plans as an essential process in your planning and evaluation cycles and not as something imposed from outside. A good inspection will recognise the strengths you already know about, but also help you identify and remedy weaknesses in your provision.

You can read a great deal more about action plans in 'Action Plans: A Guide for Private, Voluntary and Independent Providers of Nursery Education', published by the DfEE and the Centre for Research in Early Childhood, Worcester College of Higher Education. You can obtain this document, free of charge, by phoning 0345 43 345 or writing to DfEE Freepost, London W1E 2DE.

This essential document not only tells you what should go into an action plan, but also gives you some sample action plans and discusses how an action plan should be implemented.

IN CONCLUSION

A well managed setting is one in which responsibilities are known; lines of communication are clear and open; staff feel some 'ownership' of the setting; the day and year run smoothly; parents know who to talk to about what; and children are involved in purposeful play as they interact with one another and with the adults. People who work in the setting are treated respectfully and their contribution is explicitly recognised. They know what they are supposed to do and have had a say in deciding key issues. The users of the setting are also treated respectfully; their views are sought and they, too, feel a sense of ownership of the setting.

Good management starts with a clear appreciation of where the setting is and where it wants to move to. Self-appraisal is the starting point of the ongoing process of evaluation and improvement and each inspection and action plan builds on what has gone before. The initial self-appraisal, talked about at the start of this chapter, is, however, not a one-off activity. At each point that some change is made, according to the action plan, the setting needs to carry out a self-appraisal and this may result in changes being made to the proposed plans set out in the action plan.

Settings can be confident that, if their aim is continually to improve the quality of education and care on offer, they will move ahead. They also need to remember, however, that change is slow and that it needs to be carefully managed. As **Pascal and Bertram** (1997) put it:

'Effective action planning will be a key element in your success.'

Start your self-appraisal tomorrow!

REFERENCE

Pascal, C. and Bertram, T., 'Action Plans: A Guide for Private, Voluntary and Independent Providers of Nursery Education', DfEE and Centre for Research in Early Childhood, Worcester College of Higher Education, 1997.

INDEX